"…..ohh, but listen"

Written by Chris Nickolay.

ISBN 978-1-0687157-1-6

Printed by ExWhyZed Print, Colchester – exwhyzed.com

Cover design by Lucy Cook

Logo design by Martin Nickolay-Blake

Contents

I have had so much help and support in the long process of completing this work. So, thank you to:

AF for early help and inspiration.

Ashley and Susan for hearing me read early on and for both of them proofing the first draft – Susan doing so in the midst of her illness and ending.

Claudio, Cliff and Howard for reading, critiquing and encouraging as I wrote.

Dana for excellent typesetting.

Ian for a final read through and careful correction.

Lucy for a beautiful cover.

Katherine for her early aid and encouragement to think.

The late Marcus Borg for his conceptual brilliance.

Mike at ExWhyZed printing for doing what he does so well.

Owen for filming so beautifully.

Richard for diligent correcting.

Tim, our neighbour, for knowing the bible so well and being open hearted.

Walter Wink for daring to challenge traditional narratives and making me laugh.

and to GoFundMe supporters who made the printing possible:

Anonymous x 4 - you know who you are

Claudio

Cliff

Dan and Norma

David

Gary

Harry

Howard

Ian

Jean

Lou

M.A. Walker

Martin (you know who you are!)

Paul S

Sarah

Stefan

Terrance

These thankyous remind me that everything, for me, happens in community even when the work feels lonely.

4

Prologue

This book is an imaginative reweaving of some stories that are part of a tradition that flows through our year, seasons and culture – whether we believe in or identify with them or not. They are recorded, in many versions of a book called the bible. I am aware that even writing 'bible' may cause some possible readers to stop. Please don't – this is not at all what you might expect.

After living with these stories and their formation for twelve years or so I discovered that there was more to consider. There were still emerging quandaries. Conversations with friends and collaborators led me to realise that the stories are better seen through the lens of myth. Instead of saying 'these are just other versions of things that are already known and set' we can listen to or read them in a different way. This can be a difficult thing to do but is definitely worth it. In this way we might possibly discover much more than if we treat the stories as fact or formed belief. Liminal moments might be gently encountered as we wait, wonder, hover and, maybe, step. A surprise, undirected encounter with something existential could occur. These might seem like big promises but there's something here of the always exciting and inviting 'once upon a time'.

Myth has come to mean untrue, devalued like so many traditional stories. However, that, in itself, is untrue. Myths can draw our gaze to a panorama of possible truths and alternate realities. In myths, characters, whilst individuals, are often also more. They can indicate something universal. Often they are big archetypes - heroic, tragic and traditionally gendered. Here the archetypes are those found in largely ordinary lives - even traditionally significant players are just everyday individuals touched by greater circumstances or realities; not special or unique. If this wasn't so, how could we genuinely learn from what their lives might reveal? Here the archetypes whilst sometimes painful or vivid are also subtle and gentle.

In these stories I lift up voices that, in different ways and for different reasons, have been hidden, denied, neglected or altered in conventional tellings. There are voices here of children, women and men, from the marginalised, criminalised, dismissed, ignored and maligned. There are voices here, too, of characters that we maybe thought we knew.

As with all of *Story Works* publications, everything is written to be read out loud to others – if you choose.

But first, a story.

Imagine, if you will, a long bowed beach of pale sand backed by dunes spiky with marram grass. In the distance but not too far away high mountains in a pale blue sky. Cold. There's an onshore wind that cuts and chills but is so much calmer than the night just gone. In the stormed darkness great bells had tolled again and again and, as the dawn lightened, people walked through the dunes and onto the beach singly, in clinging pairs or close huddled groups. Now they can see the summoning bells roped high in their supports to the leaning great mast of the biggest ship they have ever seen – almost the length of the beach. The vessel is broken, split like a barrel dropped high from a warehouse bay. A wreck is a terrible sadness.

Nudged to and fro by flowing ripples are straw-wrapped parcels. Further out are black, red and brown chests bound with iron, brass and silver bands, rivets and locks. People splash and hurry to retrieve the wreck's gifts – there seems to be nobody to claim them. Picking up the parcels, now clearly bottle shaped, and dragging or lugging the chests, they hurry to where the beach is above the returning tide. Then their glee is frozen by the return of the bell's boom. This time it's not the rocking waves but two gowned women pulling and releasing, pulling and releasing thick red ropes swaying the bells. Before it was a distress alarum, now it's a warning call to stop. These are people prepared to listen, and they pause. The two women tie off the ropes. They climb down the broken ship like it's a peculiar ladder and wade into the sea. They pull hoods over their heads as they come and they begin to sing. Gulls swoop and echo the singing. Way behind the dunes dogs, hackles up, raise their voices in a dawn howling and the people on the beach find that they have gathered, holding hands and begin singing, humming notes without words. Skylarks rise early in meadows a way back. A child walks towards the women ignoring a parent's tug. She bends, picks up a parcel and peels away the straw. She sits, a greenish glass bottle in her lap, long against her small body. She looks into the bottle, tilts her head, leans forward cradling the treasure and says to nobody in particular, 'Ohh listen, there are voices.' Hearing this the two women grasp each other's arms as if to steady themselves and then, pulling the hoods off their heads and shaking their hair, they gesture for people to walk into the shelter of the dunes where, in a wide circle, they all sit in a deep, soft-sanded and wind-free hollow. So far only the child has spoken, and she still holds the bottle. The two women have, momentarily, bowed their heads as if resting. When they look up one is smiling and the other has tears running down her cheeks – again, they lean into each other like two windblown silver birches. They tell a story. The ship that they piloted was carrying every story, every myth and tale ever told in any language. The cargo had been kept, free to everyone who sought, in a great library in warm hills near a harbour on an island far away. Then war, ignorance and greed had come, and it breathed fire. Escape was necessary and of immense risk and sadness. The women were the last of a crew not killed by storm, hunger or illness. Their purpose? To find a haven for the myths, stories and tales and build them a new home. This beach, it seemed, was the end of their journey and travail. The women stopped. Someone passed them a stone bottle of wine and they drank and smiled. It was delicious and warm. An older woman in the circle stood leaning on a smoothed driftwood pole. She gazed around her friends and neighbours seeking their eyes. She looked finally at the child still cradling the bottle who, smiling, held it up to her. Taking it, the old woman said, "I think the myths, stories and tales have found their home. We'd best get them into the warm." Everybody smiled, some wept and the two women from the ship looked as if they would burst with joy as they grinned and cried at the same time.

Days later, when the beach was cleared and the precious cargo rescued, some villagers of all ages met in the candle lit corner of a tented cavern, a temporary archive, made of sailcloth and cut masts from the ruins of the ship. Here there were caskets and chests laid out on planks. One of the guardian women chose a chest, it had a label spelling Biblos. She pressed a raised brass heart in the centre of the top of the lid. It opened a little after the single click of a catch released. She asked a child to help lift the lid up and back. Inside, the chest seemed deeper than it had looked resting on the planks. It was filled with layers of snugly fitting trays. Each of these held carefully packed scrolls - some of the scrolls were in small, rectangular, lidded glass boxes tied closed with gold wire. As it was opened those closest felt their faces brushed by whispers. Startled, they touched to feel what might be there but, oddly, there was nothing. After a few minutes of people lifting and looking at scrolls and boxes the woman closed the lid.

Here, now, are some of what later wonderers discovered, liked, read and told from this particular chest...

A note from an archivist in the new library

Sometimes, with these stories, the transcriber of the scrolls from earlier originals has written an instruction as to who is speaking - so, for example, 'Miryam speaks'. A way had to be found to enable you, a reader, to, occasionally, feel the gaze of a story member on your face, their words into your ears - directly from their when into your now which come, as some letter writers say, 'with kind regards', a gentle look.

The Stories

Miryam

Waking

Once upon a time there was a young woman, let's call her Miryam. In the night warmth of the sun's heat releasing from the walls of her home, she woke dreaming someone had touched her belly with a flat, gentle hand. Her heart was going fast but, somehow, she wasn't afraid. There had been a voice, soft, a breath near her ear, tickling. Dream or not? As you will know, at waking moments, it can be hard to tell, but she had the shocking certainty that something else was in her body and, in the most peculiar way, it had a purpose for which she was responsible. She also knew then that she was, for much of this task, going to be alone. She knew that she was also going to have to be very, very careful. It couldn't be a secret but whatever happened because of who she told, she had to hold tight. How did she know? There'd been that whisper, whether from outside or in, and what was in her, yes, a body growing towards being a person, was, for a short while, going to need extraordinarily fierce protection. It was going to cost, but somehow, the task itself would strengthen her. In the morning she would have to begin and tell Yosef. He was going to find it harder, but men always do.

It is a bright, clear, high sky day, full of sunshine. The air smells of the bark of trees – warm, spicy. A young woman, Rebekah, dressed in a long brown tunic and grey shawl stands, shading herself for a moment, under a tree whose branches arch low over her head. Doves peck at spilled seeds on the red, dusty ground. Suddenly, there's a shout and the birds fly up in a flapping, clattering cloud. They circle and land on a red roof top and in a light green, spiky tree. The woman, startled, grips her hands together, frightened, nails digging into the base of her fingers.

Rebekah speaks:

"I work in the house of Joachim and Hannah. It's usually peaceful and happy but something bad is happening. Yosef, who's going to marry Miryam, their daughter, has crashed out of the front door of the house. I've never seen him so angry. Miryam has run out after him, crying, her hands grasping towards him. He spits words, 'you can't be pregnant – we're not married. What have you done? Who have you been with? You've broken everything'. Miryam stops, looks straight at him without lowering her head, and says, 'I told you, I don't know, I dreamed, as if I was awake and something, I don't know, spoke to me. You know this happens to people! It told me I would be pregnant, and the baby would be extraordinary – maybe the one we've all been waiting for. I don't know what to think. I'm scared. I don't know what to do. You said you had a dream too. So, please, don't be so vile. What did your dream tell you to do?' Yosef is still – I just hear him say – 'I have to marry you, whatever.' Oh, they've seen me".

Rebekah ducks her head and turns away, stepping hurriedly down the path between low broken rocky walls to the town. Who will she tell?

Miryam looks at Yosef – "we have to tell mum and dad – I know, he really might beat or kill me or, at least, send me away. I'm scared. I need time to think – I'll go away myself. I can stay with Elizabeth. She'll look after me." Yosef just stares. He knows her mum and dad will find it hard to believe her story, to believe it wasn't his fault, him that got her pregnant. Was it when they lay in the long grass and touched each other?

They find Hannah and Joachim sitting in a leafy shelter in the garden – the sweet perfume of the flowers in the trees anoints the air. It's quiet. Yosef lets Miryam speak first – he is afraid about how angry they are going to be. He forgets to protect her.

Miryam starts by telling them about her waking from maybe a dream. Then, breathing slowly, she tells them that she is pregnant – she just knows she can feel it. Joachim tightens his hands into fists and says nothing. Hannah wrings the cloth of her dress in her hands and cries, rending, silently – the heavy drops of tears stain her dress.

Then her dad shouts, "How could you? Don't tell me you had a dream – I don't believe you. Go, go – do as you say, go and see your cousin Elizabeth – I don't want you here. Go away!" He wants to beat her but can't. Then, arms around each other, leaning together, Joachim and Hannah leave the shelter of the garden and go indoors. Miryam sobs and grips her tummy, hurting more than she has ever known – like a deep bruise inside. Yosef says nothing – useless.

Much later Rebekah comes quietly through the garden to the kitchen; her usual smile becomes a sneer when she sees Miryam sitting picking grit out of lentils.

A ruined scarf

Miryam needed some cloth for a new dress before going away. Her mum goes with her to the market in the town. Miryam has covered her head with a soft, long, wide, white scarf. They walk out of the house and down a path between sheltering rows of trees. The leaves on the trees are silvery green and grey – they smell tangy and peppery in the warm air. She hears a thrush singing a stream of notes in the garden behind the trees. Her heart lifts.

As they get to the bright market Miryam notices that people are staring at her – some are pointing and laughing. Who's told people she's pregnant? At the stall selling cloth, she quickly buys what she wants – the cloth is soft, heavy and pale blue. As she turns to go home something hits her on the head; purple juice stains her white scarf – somebody has thrown fruit at her. More is thrown – it hurts.

She runs with her mum down the street into the synagogue hoping that stones aren't thrown. Hannah begs the priest to let them shelter until it's safe – he says no they can't but shows them the small back door out into an alley. Even there people shout at them. They have to run, Miryam sobbing all the way home almost falling onto the hard ground.

When her dad hears what has happened, he is so angry that Hannah has to wrap her arms round him and grip to stop him running to the market with his stick and beating people who hurt Miryam. That evening Hannah quietly sits and makes the dress – sometimes, again, tears drop and darken the cloth. Miryam packs her clothes.

In the morning, she eats a little bread, honey and fruit for breakfast even though her tummy still hurts. Her mum gives her a hat that's big and round to hide her face and keep the sun's heat off her head. Yosef, still not speaking to her, brings a little two wheeled wooden cart to the front of the house. It's pulled by a grey and black donkey and is ready to take her to Elizabeth's house. Her dad puts her bag into the cart and lifts her so that she sits, with her legs dangling, on the edge of the open back. The wood is rough, a bit spiky and warm on her legs. She has her hat on her head and sits looking down so that nobody can see her. Yosef taps the donkey with a stick and the cart moves, bumpily, down the track from her home. Her mum and dad stand very still watching her go – they haven't hugged her. She is the saddest she has ever been.

She is sleepy in the warm air. She holds the side of the cart with one hand and leans back against her bag and a sack of gifts and food for Elizabeth. Soothed with the gentle bumping she drifts and dozes for all of the journey. She wakes when the bumping stops. She hears the sound of a hoe chopping into the earth and hitting stones. Yosef helps her down from the cart and lifts out her bag and the gifts. Elizabeth, who is pregnant, has a very round tummy. She wipes her face on a cloth and walks, slowly, smiling, down a stony path towards Miryam who runs to her cousin who holds her tightly. She cries again, quietly. Yosef says nothing, not even goodbye and turns the cart around and leaves for home – back to Miryam's parents. Elizabeth, puzzled, picks up the bag and Miryam carries the gifts; they go into the creamy white house where Elizabeth lives with her husband Zechariah. They drink cool water and wine. Elizabeth tells Miryam - "You know I've never had a baby, never thought I would, so I don't know what it feels like, but the funny, odd thing is when I saw you, I felt the baby in me wriggle and jump. My heart beat faster." Miryam, reaching out, holds her cousin's hand and says, "I'm pregnant too" and tells her everything that has happened. Elizabeth says nothing – she's not upset or angry – she smiles. Miryam feels safe but wonders why her cousin's baby jumped.

Goodbye, hello and new danger

Elizabeth speaks:

"Miryam is leaving me today. She has to go back home – to be there before her baby is born. I am both worried and happy for her – it's so hard being pregnant but when almost everybody seems to hate her, well I think she is brave and strong even if she doesn't feel like that. I have put soft cushions in a little cart with a roof for her journey home. Yosef hasn't come; I could happily slap him for his meanness and cruelty – he dreamed too but just ignores it. How he ever goes to synagogue when he has no faith, no kindness – what did the prophet say: 'G'd[1] has told us what is good – do justice, love kindness and walk humbly'[2]. Bah – what a stupid man. I am sad to see her go. I know what her dream said but I wonder what is going to happen to our children as they grow. She sent me a message with my neighbour back from market and said her mum hugged her when she got home, and her dad smiled and cried to see her, but Yosef stayed hiding in his workshop. Rebekah has gone. Hannah was so cross with her that she sent her back to her family in the town. She begged to stay and say sorry to Miryam, but Hannah said no – go, go away. Miryam has decided just to stay at home for the weeks before the baby comes – she is keeping away from unkind and spiteful people – well, apart from Yosef. She eats and drinks, rests, walks in the garden – she doesn't go into the town where people threw things at her. Her baby grows and she says that, despite everything, she feels peaceful whilst she waits for the boy to be born whose name she already knows. I look forward to our babies meeting."

Miryam speaks:

"I thought you should hear my voice now instead of other people telling you my story. Today I'm sitting in a cool kitchen quietly cutting vegetables for supper – leeks, onions, cucumber. My mum and dad are now just as I hoped they might be and look after me – our love as a family has helped us to stop hurting one another. Yosef, though, still barely talks to me – I know he's hurt but I am surprised at how selfish he is being. He only speaks when he wants something – a drink or some food. He never touches me. Right now, I hear him calling my dad – what can he want? He sounds upset, angry. Is it about me again? Sometimes I wish he wasn't here! What's going on? He's waving a piece of paper at my dad – it's torn at one corner, like he's pulled it off a wall or door. He shouts, 'look, look what it says. What are we going to do?' My dad tells us what it says. He rages as he speaks. 'All Jews have to go back to the place where they were born so that the Romans, and their servants in the Temple, can count us and get more money from us.'

Dad uses a word I have never heard him say before about the Romans and wishes them dead. Yosef looks desperate. 'I don't know what to do. All my work is here. The road to Bith Lehem³ is lonely and dangerous and – look, look at her, how can she travel all that way? I know she's my wife, but I don't want to take her, but I have to. I've promised to look after her until this damned baby is born.' My mum gasps at what he has said. Dad stares at him – I think he might grab him and shake him in fury. Me? At last, I see that he really wants me gone. I find my voice – 'we have to go. If we don't the soldiers will come for us and that will be much worse. I don't want to go all that way especially with you being so horrible. So, you don't want to be near me but here we are and you're going to have to put up with me and me with you.' He looks back at me – I can see that he wants to shout at me but doesn't dare in front of mum and dad. Just now I really don't like him. He says, 'I'll go and take you to be counted, but once we get there and you have the baby, whatever he's called, I'm going to leave you to do whatever you want but I don't want you coming back with me.' There is only silence in the room. I leave Yosef with his anger and shame and go to my room where I sleep alone. I am going to pack everything I need to live in a new place. I pack the small sharp knife dad gave me for cooking – I might need it for more than cooking."

Leaving and a journey

Miryam speaks:

"The next day is cloudy and cold. It's early in the morning. Goats and sheep are bleating and coughing nearby – their bells clang softly. The memory of the terrible things that Yosef said sits like a rock inside me, squashing the happy weight of the baby. Dad and Yosef have decided its best just to take a donkey and not a cart as well – the roads are going to be rocky and rough and, if needed, it is easier to hide with just a donkey.

The soft, grey and black, sad-faced creature is already loaded with the rusty red cloth bags holding my clothes and other things. I'm wearing a thick brown dress and coat without buttons. Nobody has spoken about Yosef's angry words. Now we have to say goodbye – how can I? This is my home – there is no home with this scowling man. I don't want to cry again but as mum and dad wrap their arms round me, I do. I don't know if I'll see them again. Dad gently lifts me on to the donkey; his arms are thick and strong. He strokes my head and quietly says goodbye again. I am going to be quiet now to help me bear the pain."

Yosef holds the rough rope tied to the donkey's bridle. Miryam gets as comfortable as is possible – the seat is hard even with a blanket. The blanket reminds her of when it covered her legs as she sat in the garden. Miryam's back quickly aches, her tummy is stretched, and her bottom is sore. How can she ask Yosef to stop when she needs the toilet?

The sun is hot. The road smells of the dung and urine of animals.

Miryam hopes the baby doesn't come when they are travelling. She has to be on the donkey or walking and then sleeping on the blanket on the ground for five days.

The donkey plods with clipping hooves out of the town up a hill – its head hangs and nods. Miryam wants to sleep but can't – she might fall off. Her lips are dry – her eyes itch with dust. She wants to ask Yosef if he meant what he said about leaving her, but he stares ahead, not looking at her, it seems not caring. Miryam sips water from a clay bottle wrapped in cloth tied by a leather thong to the side of the seat. They go a long way without stopping. As the dusk light softens and darkens Yosef sees a large and flat smooth rock – a good place to halt and rest. There's a little stream splashing and flowing noisily a few steps down a gravelly slope from the rock – it helps the air feel cooler. Yosef stops, ties the rope to a small thorny tree, pats the donkey's head and helps Miryam down. She is stiff and sore and quickly has to go behind a rock before she wets herself. Yosef turning away leads the donkey to the stream – it stands in the water and has a long dribbling drink.

Yosef looks up as he hears the sound of several animals walking along the track above where they sit – there is a man leading a tethered line of donkeys loaded with bags. Another person walks behind using a long thick stick to tap the animals when they try to stop to munch a plant.

The man pauses, looks, and shakes his head; the line stops as he sits to rest and drink from the neck of an animal skin bulging with water. He waves to Yosef who doesn't wave back. Miryam comes out from behind the rock.

The man speaks:

"Oh no. I really wanted to stop here for the night – now we'll have to walk more. Why are these people here – I always think this place is just mine. She's pregnant. It's so dangerous here. What is he doing? He's laid out one blanket with some food and drink by it and now he's moving away and sitting on another blanket with his back to the woman. What is the matter here? Maybe I'll see them in the next town if they get there."

The little caravan of donkeys trudges off in the quickly deepening grey dusk, leaving Miryam and Yosef settling silently and sadly for the night. Miryam is awake for a little while hoping Yosef will become kinder and talk to her. As her eyelids drop shut, she wonders whether he'll come and lie close to her – if for nothing else than to be warmer. She misses his touch – she remembers lying in warm, long grass with him.

A closed door

Miryam speaks:

"I'm cold. I'm shivering under this blanket. My hair is wet – is it rain or dew? Oh, I have another blanket on me – I thought it felt heavier. Yosef must have covered me in the night. For the first time in days, I smile a little – even a tiny kindness helps – but he's still silent, so what's the point? How can he keep being so angry; this isn't the gentle, funny Yosef I fell in love with – nor is he the person my parents chose for me – how could he be? Well, do you know, I don't care. I'll ignore him and wait for him to go and then get on with being mother to this baby in any way I can."

Miryam goes behind the rock again and then washes her hands and face in the cold stream water. Her face feels smooth and shiny. After a little breakfast of bread and dates and water they begin to walk – it's too soon for Miryam to ride, she'll save that for when she is even more tired.

This was the story for four more days. Sometimes Miryam had to stop and lie under a tree in the middle of the day – if she didn't, she might fall with tiredness. Yosef hated stopping and he still spoke only a few words.

Miryam speaks:

"Finally, we've arrived in Bith Lehem. I can feel my baby heavier and heavier pushing downwards. Even walking is hard now. I just want

23

him to be born. As we go into the streets Yosef turns to speak to me – more than a few blunt, careless words. I almost don't recognise his voice speaking without anger – I don't hurt inside when he speaks. He says that he has a cousin here in the town where we might stay. Oh – I hope so – somewhere comfortable and warm with more than bread and dates to eat. He walks us through the tiny streets until he sees the door he knows. He knocks and it is opened by a woman – she looks like Yosef. He says hello and she smiles and then she sees me and her smile turns into a look like she has smelt something disgusting. 'You can stay but she can't – she can sleep in the street where rubbish belongs.' Yosef suddenly looks surprised, even shocked. It's not only what she's said but it's like he's seen in her face what I see in his. He steps back as if she's hit him, hard. 'No thank you. Goodbye.'

He turns round to me. His cousin stares at him and bangs the door hard shut. 'We will have to keep looking and asking.'

'Excuse me, we are looking for somewhere to sleep – my wife is pregnant and needs to rest. Do you know anywhere?'

'Why should I help you – you're probably a thief or drunk. Go away'.

'Hello. Excuse me. We are here to be counted and need somewhere to sleep. My wife is pregnant. Can you help us?'

'Don't come near me – how dare you. Go away'. 'Hello. Excuse me. My name is Yosef. We are here to be counted. My wife is pregnant, and we need somewhere to sleep. Do you know anywhere?' The man spoken to pauses with his line of donkeys, turns. He smiles – 'well now, hello again. You were that unfriendly traveller resting by the stream on the road and now you ask for help. I'm glad you're safe.' Yosef bows his head slightly – 'sorry, it wasn't a good day.' The man nods. 'Well, I can't help you – I'm just travelling through – but that place over there, the Khan[4], selling wine and food, they might have somewhere. Ask them.' 'Thank you for your kindness – blessings on your journey.'

Yosef looks at me with a tiny smile and then, as if he remembers to be hurt and angry, turns away. We cross the street, and Yosef goes in to ask.

Rest and new life

Miryam speaks:

"At last, we have somewhere warm and sheltered from the sky and dust and bright heat. Grasping a rough post holding the roof I slowly sit and lean back into thick hay tucked in a corner. Yosef cleans, rubs our strong donkey with hay and makes sure it can reach water and food. He goes outside to fill a bucket from the well in the courtyard between our building and the house. He brings me some and then lies down in the straw near to where the donkey is sitting. My legs ache, my back and bottom are sore, my tummy feels stretched tight like it can't grow anymore. My eyes close in the soft dark; I sleep quickly."

"I wake, it's still dark. I have the worst pain I have ever had – low down in my tummy. The straw is wet. I don't want to wake Yosef, but the hurting makes me yelp as it bites hard. He stands, brightens the light in a lantern and comes to me – he looks frightened but still just stands, watching. Now I'm angry and I don't care – 'if you won't help go, go and find a woman who can – I knew you'd be useless'. He runs out. Suddenly I am completely alone with just a soft yellow light. Supposing he's actually gone – he said he'd leave me; maybe he's just run away. Then, oh thank G'd, I hear the sound of hurrying, scuffing feet and a voice, Yosef's, saying, 'quick, please quick, she's in here'. Then he's back and there's a woman with him – thick shining black hair, a smile that says, 'you're safe, I'll help, don't worry'. She smells like the garden at home – warm flowers and that spicy bark. When that angel, yes, I think it was, spoke to me in a dream he said nothing about the pain – if he'd been a she maybe it would have been different! Pain and rest, pain and rest. Yosef just watches; the woman, Riva, holds my hand, rubs my back, talks softly and understandingly, gives me water." "Pain and rest, pain and rest – now less rest and more, quicker, sharper pain. Riva turns to Yosef. 'You, go to the house, ask them to heat water – we'll need it soon'. I had shown her where, in my bags, I'd carefully packed clean, white cloth – ready for the baby coming. For a few moments the squalls of pain stop and then all I can do is let my muscles work – it's like, oh no, the shame, I need to go behind the rock to empty myself, please, that can't happen. I'm shouting, telling G'd I don't want this baby, make it all stop. Yosef is back. I thrust my arm, my hand up towards him, staring at him. He hesitates and then grips it like he'll never, ever let go again – he smiles and cries at the same time. At last, he's with me – again."

"Suddenly the sharpest pains end and there's a small high crying and Riva, dear Riva, lifts the baby, wraps him in a cloth and gives him to me. I had wondered, would this baby seem different from other babies? I hold him while Riva cleans him, ties off the cord that joined him to me and, no, he's just a baby – exquisite, vulnerable, complete, loved, present and perfect. In the beginning, the Book says, there was only potential."

1 I have chosen to use G'd instead of including an 'o' 'for two reasons. In some Jewish traditions, but not all, the name of G'd is given great respect and should not be reproduced in any setting where it can be erased. This does not, necessarily, apply when the name, or title is written in a language other than Hebrew. Nevertheless, I like the idea of a deep and simple respect for what I think of as the presence of the divine in, and accessible to, everybody. I also think that, in our culture, the word God is, in many people's minds and religious traditions symbolised, imagined as male and probably old and white; G'd can be felt or filled with any or many identities. It's a delicate shift. When you read it out loud or to yourself just say 'God'.

2 This is part of a quotation from the Old Testament of the bible – the book of Micah, chapter 6, verse 8. It is used a lot in Christian social justice settings.

3 Bith Lehem or Bethlehem means in Hebrew, 'The house – of bread'.

4 A 'Khan' or caravanserai was accommodation for travellers. There would be space for animals, sleeping space, ritual and religious areas and, sometimes, places to buy food and drink and to trade.

The poorest men

Sheep move on the dark hillside like clusters of small, luminous clouds. Sheep herders sit on the ground around a fire, eating bread, soft lentils, and onions, drinking water. Their wide hoods are over their heads – the air is cold on their skin and smells of sweet wood smoke. The sky is dark blue, almost black, filled with sharp, bright stars – cut jewels on velvet.

Suddenly they sit up, stop eating. They've heard a bell, on an animal's neck, that they don't recognise and hooves scrambling on stones. They reach for their thick staves, hands on knives. Up the sloping path on a curve round a slope of hill comes the trader from the town, leading his line of donkeys – his son, almost unseen in the dusk, is walking at the end of the line. The trader comes on, stops when he sees the circle of alert, watchful, dangerous men. They relax. They know him – he often comes by although, today, he's late. He ties the strong leather lead from the front donkey's neck around a rock and puts it carefully on the ground and comes to the yellow fire. The shepherds offer him and his son food and drink from what they have. He thanks them. "Well,", he says, "have you heard the news?"

"What news, we've not been near the town for days. We can't leave the sheep," says the youngest shepherd.

The trader looks around the circle of strong, brown, warm faces – eyes reflecting flames. "I've heard that the great promise has come true. You know – about the one who is going to save us, he's come, he's been born." The shepherds are quiet, even the air seems still. They wait for more. "Look", the trader says, "on my way from Naz'-a-reth I passed a couple on the road. She was big and pregnant and separate from the man with her. He seemed angry and ignored her – unfriendly to me. Later, in the town, I saw them again – I'd heard a woman's voice shouting, spitting words and a door slamming. The man asked me about somewhere to sleep for the woman and him. I showed them old David's Khan." The trader pauses and drinks. Still the shepherds are quiet, waiting. "You know, my days are long and sometimes not much happens so I get curious, even a bit nosey. Where I was staying, in the evening after food, I asked if anyone had heard anything about the woman or the man. Someone, a woman, serving, turned, and said, 'I heard from the sister of the woman who slammed the door that the man is a cousin called Yosef and that she'd barred the pregnant woman from staying in her home.' A man spoke next. 'I'm here to be counted but my friend, Saul, from Naz'-a-reth, told me about his friend's sister, Rebekah, who used to work for the mother of the pregnant woman, she's named Miryam. Anyway, he told me that Miryam had a dream, and an angel told her that she would have a baby who would be the one to save us.' The trader is still. "At first, I thought, here we go again, another story to be hopeful about and then it breaks and there's only disappointment, but the man was definite. I asked around some more that evening. It seems the woman, Miryam, was attacked, and might have been killed, in her town. The husband, if he is, also had a dream telling him to marry and protect Miryam – he didn't want to, which is maybe why they don't seem to get on. Again, Saul told me this. Look", the trader says, "the prophecy is not for a warrior or a king like that mamzer[5] Herod but of a baby, a baby, who is or will become the one – for all and each of us. Before I left the town I walked to David's – from outside I heard a baby crying; it seems he's been born."

The youngest shepherd gasped and stood. His heart was beating hard, fast. He spoke, almost singing, repeating, *"oh Bith-Lechem in Y'hudah, you are amongst the smallest of all the places – yet from you will come a ruler who will shepherd my people"*[6] Two of the other shepherds stood and put their arms around his shoulders almost holding him up. "We must go", one said. "Some of us must stay to guard the sheep but the rest of us, come, let's go." Two older, slower men said that they'd stay.

The others wrapped some bread and fruit in a cloth, picked up their thick, strong staves, thanked and said goodbye to the trader who, smiling, went back to his donkeys and journey.

They began to walk, fast, down the hill. They hoped they wouldn't be seen – to leave sheep was a crime. The shepherd at the front heard singing – it was the youngest shepherd again, almost running – it was a song from the Book - "*Haaah, workers who sow with tears will reap with songs of joy. If we go out weeping, carrying seed to sow we will come home singing songs of joy, our arms full of sheaves*"[7] – then, all singing, they flew down the path.

They came to the edge of the town and slowed. They didn't want soldiers, guards or priests to see them. They walked, close together, holding hands, to the Khan of the man David. They were strong men, used to living in the hills protecting the sheep, driving off wolves and men, even poorer than them, trying to steal animals – now they felt funny, shy, a bit afraid – of a baby? They stepped softly through the gateway and, ahead of them, a yellow light glowed from the low building opposite the main building. They nudged the younger one forward, laughing nervously, "Go on, go on, you go in first, we're too ugly – don't want to frighten the baby." They followed him in – almost stumbling. Yosef looked up, surprised, ready, now, to protect Miryam. She quickly covered herself as she'd been feeding her baby – the shepherds turned away for a moment. Then she, smiling at Yosef and then at the shepherds, said, "Please come in – you are welcome." They sat, offered food to the couple, who were hungry, and waited. Miryam gently folded the blanket back from the face of the baby so that they could see.

The youngest shepherd said, "We are sorry to unsettle your rest, but we had to come when we heard what people have said, about you, the baby, your dream. Sorry, sorry."

Miryam said, "You are welcome. If my dream is true, then you are the people for whom my baby has been born. I don't know what is going to happen but if the love that I feel for him is ever given back to the world, then there is hope for everyone." The youngest shepherd, bewildered, crying softly, asked to touch the head of the baby – they then each did this, thanked Miryam and Yosef and, in wonder, went back to the hills.

5 *Mamzer – Hebrew for 'bastard' with an implication of being the child of incest*

6 *This is a reference to the book of Micah chapter 5 verse 2.*

7 *This is a reference to Psalm126 5:6. Here is a link to a recording of a cantor, a synagogue singer, made in the early 20th century just to give a flavour of the sound of psalm singing in Hebrew – this is the same psalm: https://youtu. be/I_4naDpm6WE*

A special day

Miryam is happy. She walks up the sloping dusty street staying in the shade of sandy coloured houses, sheltering from the sharp, bright sunlight that's hard on her eyes. Her baby is asleep, tied closely to her front in a wide band of soft white cloth wrapped around her middle and her shoulders - safe, now. Yosef, next to her, is smiling. Over his shoulder, on a broad strap and bouncing a little on his left hip is a big bag made of goat's skin. He carries some food for the day - a crusty, chunky piece of bread, dried fish, olives, and drink in a clay bottle. There are two other, small, precious bundles. When the traders from the king visited, they brought gifts. In a little brown cloth bag tied with a leather string is one of the coins they gave, gold - not Roman - to buy two pigeons as a gift for the Temple. In a tiny glass bottle, wrapped in big leaves, is some of the oil they brought, frankincense. Yosef and Miryam hope to burn it and so make the air full of perfume, rising up, like the scent of angels.

It's a special day for this mum and dad. They are taking their baby to the Temple to say, "here, G'd, is our first child. We remember when all our families were slaves and then escaped across the river and through the desert. Please, keep him safe." As they walk Miryam remembers the dream she had - was it still true? She has had no more dreams telling her what to do. Maybe one is enough.

They arrive at the great steps up to the high square stone gateway into the Temple. It's so big, hard, like a fort in the desert - Miryam, and Yosef, for a moment, are scared. They stop, rest before climbing through thick, pushing crowds. Starting up, Miryam, holding Yosef's hand, puts her other arm across the baby, like a shield. The air is full of the sounds and stinks of animals - lambs, pigeons, sheep, goats, cattle - and of fires burning and smoking. Halfway up, a golden brightness flashes off the metal, bronze, on the pillars holding the gate; Miryam trips, Yosef grabs her arm, holds her and they smile again. Their baby wriggles and puts a tiny hand out into the air.

Earlier in the day a woman called Anna woke in her little room in the Temple. It was one of the days when she wouldn't eat until the evening - she'd just drink, be quiet a lot and say some prayers gently, alone. In between sleeping and waking she felt sadness climbing up in her from low down inside. When she stood, she almost fell over as she felt it rising, it was like an empty wave flooding over her, grey, forcing her to hold tight, flat handed, to the wall. She was a very old person and sometimes this happened. She sat down on her little bed. She needed to go to her favourite place - now. Walking on the cold stone floor, her feet, in thin sandals, hurt. She came to steps and looked down so as not to trip. She thought, 'my I'm old; I'm 84 and still here'. She remembers the Temple being built and wondered how many people have walked here - in and out, up and down.

She stands close to the gate that leads to the next gate, that leads to the heart of the Temple, the secret place. She can't go through. Here, though, she feels so close to love, to G'd, and love, G'd feels so close to her that her heart beats faster. Her eyes sparkle. The bossy priest with the thick robes and oily hair glares at her – "how dare you stand there; what do you know; get away!" She just stands still, her feet aching but flat and strong on the stone - stone cut, shaped, laid and fitted by people forgotten, but whose hands are remembered in the building - stone prayers.

She turns away to a quiet corner where jugs of water stand with cups for thirsty visitors. She pours, sits on a wonky three-legged wooden stool and sips. She rests her eyes. A cry makes her jump. She looks to the gate to the outside. There's Simeon, her old, old friend. He is so quiet and gentle. HIs body curves towards the ground now, often hurting - part of him wants to lie down somewhere warm, soft and safe, close his eyes and sleep, sleep and not wake, to end. But he's waiting.

What's happened? He's dropped his black knobbly thorn tree stick, smooth where he grips it, and he's smiling, holding a baby, its parents close by, nervous of the frail old man, a stranger. Anna, lifting the thick cloth of her skirts off the ground - it would be rubbish to trip - hurries to her friend. He's still cradling the baby so carefully a tear trickles down his brown, crinkly old skin and he doesn't wipe it away. "Anna, it's him, it's him. This is Miryam, his mother, the one we heard about, who had the dream. Anna, it's him. After all this time waiting - I know it's him." Anna's knees go soft and the man, Yosef, grips her arm at the elbow so she doesn't fall. The woman, Miryam, reaches for her hand, holds it and then, gently, lifts the baby from Simeon and gives him to Anna. Simeon has gone quiet, still, sort of inside himself.

Anna knew it was very, very dangerous to let soldiers see the baby and his mum and dad. She knew she should tell soldiers or a priest, but she doesn't. She holds the tiny thing a little more, close to her heart, gives him back, hugs Miryam, smiles at Yosef. A while after they have gone, she turns to the crowd and calls out, "he is come, the person who will help us, I have seen him, remember, be ready." Miryam heard the shout, ducked her head, and gripped her baby – "if this is part of my dream coming true, I don't like it." Anna didn't notice Simeon follow the family and whisper to Miryam who stopped, swayed, her blue scarf falling from her head, her black hair flicking across her face and, leaning against Yosef, she said 'what does he mean be ready, too, for great sadness?

A lost child in dangerous times

Once there was man called Isaac.

Isaac speaks:

"I live and work in the Temple. I remember seeing the couple, Miryam and Yosef, the parents of the child Yeshua, in the town for the festival. They had come a long way with a big crowd of people from their home. It was the first time they had made the journey, and it could be dangerous. On the roads they walked there were robbers and there were violent clashes between Romans and Zealots and other fighters. When they came into the Temple, they looked happy to be here and proud of their child. He was clever, friendly and loved by people and, of course, I had heard the stories about when he was born and the visitors who were there - the very poor shepherds who risked losing their flocks, visitors from another king who had travelled a long way angering Herod our king, a dangerous man. I had also heard about the other child, born to Miryam's cousin, Elizabeth, at almost the same time. Strange stories.

Aaaah, you see, sitting or praying or doing jobs in the Temple all day gives me almost too much time to think, wonder, and sometimes worry about how people's stories might turn out. I remember the young shepherd, I think he was one who was there just after Yeshua was born, coming to me, desperate for money to pay for his wife's medicine. I refused him and told him to pray. Sometimes I'm useless. I wonder what became of him. Maybe he went to the Zealots and helped rob a tax collector? What would I do if I had a sick wife or friend? But, as usual, I ramble and think you'll be interested.

The days after the festival are also strong in my memory. This time, I think it was two days later, Miryam and Yosef came back, and they were not smiling or happy. They looked a mixture of terrible worry, fury and, being puzzled, I spoke to them. They said that, with all of their family and friends, they had left to go home. Everybody had been up late after the festival. Most of the children had stayed with friends or family in different houses or caravanserai so they hadn't worried when they didn't see their son at the morning mealtime. They had walked, under the protection of their guards, a long way until the next mealtime when they arrived at a sheltered wadi with a pool fed by a spring. It was then, not seeing their child anywhere, that the terrible fear that all mums and dads know, began to pinch at their insides. Where was he? What had happened? They knew that they had to go back the way they had come, this time without guards to protect them - by themselves. Dangerous."

"When I saw them, it was early evening. They had walked a very, very long way in one day and they were worn out and tired with worry and fear. They were thirsty and hungry and grumpy. I thought, oh good I can help them. I had seen their child earlier, so I said, 'It's alright, I've seen him. I know where he is.' Miryam looked as if she might cry and Yosef looked like he might grab or hit me. 'where is he?' Yosef shouted. I didn't understand why he was angry - I had never been a dad - I thought I was helping. I told them, 'I saw him with a group of rabbis in the Temple courtyard about an hour ago.' Miryam grabbed my hand and gripped it tightly and then she let go and they ran off. Later, I heard what happened. Their son had started asking a rabbi some questions, listened and then asked more questions. Other rabbis joined in - they were amazed at how clever the child was; he was saying the sorts of things that only very clever grownups were supposed to know or think about. Who was G'd? Why didn't G'd help them more? Where was G'd? Why was G'd just in the temple and not everywhere? Of course, lots of adults make the very big mistake of thinking that children can only know what grownups know and can't know things for themselves - they think children have to be told everything and can't just be clever and wise. They certainly don't think children have anything to teach grownups. Rabbis, any teachers, can especially think this and be very bossy and think themselves very clever indeed. So, this talking had gone on for hours and the child was loving it. They had even stopped to share food and none, excuse me, none of my silly rabbi friends had thought to ask, wait, where are the parents of this boy? People in the courtyard had jumped when they heard a loud angry voice, 'Yeshua, what do you think you are doing, where have you been?'

I am told that, by the time Miryam and Yosef got to where Yeshua stood, most of the rabbis had stood back, trees bent in a storm. The courtyard was very quiet. It looked like Yosef would hit his son he was so angry. Miryam just grabbed her child, held him very, very tight and said, 'how dare you, how dare you frighten me, us, like this?' Yeshua didn't look a bit sorry but tried to stand straight and look at his mum and dad - this made things worse. He said, 'didn't you know I'd be here in the house of, of G'd, my father? See, I know about your dream.' People who were near said his voice sounded arrogant, almost rude, and for all of his cleverness, with no idea of the hurt and fear he'd caused. Someone said, 'typical ungrateful child.' Yosef grabbed him and pulled him from the Temple. Miryam was almost running to keep up. It was late so, again I'm told, they stayed in a small, cheap Khan. When they ate, Yosef was frowning, still angry although he occasionally looked at his child with relief and tenderness – calming down, perhaps a bit sad about grabbing and pulling him. Yeshua sat only eating little bits of food, mainly keeping his arms folded and scowling as if nobody understood him. Miryam ate and sat close to her child, her eyes red and sore. In the morning, when they left, again with no guard, Yosef walked ahead and Miryam walked with Yeshua, her arm lightly across his small shoulders. He didn't brush her off."

Later that day, when they stopped to rest, Miryam looked at Yosef, smiled and said, quietly, "I am happy that he stood, talked, asked questions and, you know, wasn't afraid."

A child gets to be a carpenter

The sunshine floated in long wide sloping beams through the sawn wood dust in the air – golden and thick at the end of the day. The boy and his dad left the work shed to go into the house to eat. There was a smell of warm bread and oil – it made them hungrier. He knew he'd been in really, really big trouble when he stayed behind in the Temple but, when they'd got home, after a day or two, his dad, Yosef, had come to him, while his mum, Miryam, smiling, was baking. Yosef said "Yeshua, it's time I told you how to cut wood and make things for us, for other people, to use in their homes, the fields, the stables, even, later, in our synagogue. Are you ready to listen, to do what I tell you, to be careful to use the tools that come from my father with his name and mine on them?" He had thought his dad would be angry with him forever, especially because his mum had been so scared and sad. So, now, he felt like the sun shone on him, warming him all over and through. He loved his dad and the tools that were part of him, named for him – things that belonged in his hands, doing what he made them do, saws, a mallet, an adze, a chisel, a rule stick and a plane. Would they, one day, have his name on them?

"When?" he had said or, really, whooped, laughing, happy. Yosef had laughed too, "Now?" and he had left the room with his son running after him, stopping to hug his mum who left floury handprints on his back. The baby in the basket on the floor smiled and giggled.

He wondered, later that day, when would his mum show him how to make bread?

Where did dad go?

Yosef always smelt of the wood he had been cutting, holding, or carrying. The scent of the sap or from the saw dust was in his skin and in the sleeves of his clothes, perfuming his sweat. When she held him, Miryam smelt the wood's different smells - one sweet and tangy, another like ripe fruit but dusty.

She kept one of his shirts in her bed. She hugged and smelt it at night. He was gone and she was alone with their children. Before he'd walked away, she'd held him the tightest she could as if she could stop him. His blanket was rolled up, the handle of a knife just sticking out, shiny and brown. His sharpest strongest axe rested on its head by the door – ready. He had been angry for weeks. The soldiers and guards kept taking money and food from everyone; the priests in the Temple helped them – even some of Miryam and Yosef's neighbours helped them hoping for a reward or to be left alone. People – children, women and men kept getting hit, pushed and cut or stabbed by the soldiers. Some died when they stood up against them, hung, tortured, on a cross by the roadside. He was so angry that he had forgotten or pushed out of his mind the dream he had had before Yeshua, his eldest son, was born Miryam tried to remind him, to get him to wait, see what happened, but he couldn't bear seeing people, friends and neighbours in pain or hunger.

He was going to the hills to live with others in caves and woods, raiding, attacking the Romans and their helpers, collaborators. He didn't want his children growing up with the soldiers and priests controlling and hurting them, keeping them and their neighbours hungry. He couldn't wait for the messiah everybody hoped would come or was here already. He left – his sons and daughter holding Miryam's legs, arms, or hands. He didn't turn, he didn't dare, he wouldn't be strong enough to go. He didn't come back to his family. Ever.

A man in the river

Once there was a man called Ephraim.

Ephraim speaks:

"Oh no, that's another stone in my sandal and they're so sharp. Why am I bothering with this? I mean my friend, Hiram, said he had heard about this man, Yohanan, who wears rough clothes and terrible sandals, who has been telling people that all their mistakes and bad things they'd done could be washed away. How washed away, I said – well, he said, in the water of the river Jordan. He said he was like a priest, one of the people working in the Temple closest to G'd, but different. That sounded a bit funny to me. I mean, who does this Yohanan think he is? Is he a messiah, someone who is supposed to beat the Romans and save us all? Or, more likely, is he just a lonely, crazy, sad person who thinks he's really important and maybe G'd.

At last, the stony path is a bit downhill and it's more dust than stones and I can see the big, wide slow-moving river in the bottom of the valley. There's already a crowd on the banks and in the water – that must be nice and cold on a hot day like today.

Everybody on the path seems excited. I suppose lots of us are having a horrible time with the Roman soldiers always on our streets and in our towns and villages with their swords and spears taking our money and food when they want. It's frightening. We want something to be hopeful about.

Talking about the soldiers I'd better be careful, there's a crowd of them by the side of the path with their brown and red cloaks, dusty helmets, short sharp swords and spears. Some are sitting, some are standing and looking at everybody, suspicious, ready to snatch or hurt anybody they don't like – child, woman or man. Hiram starts to walk more quickly – he's grinning like he just heard the best joke. He doesn't even notice the soldiers. One of them calls out – 'Oi, you with the stupid grin, what's so funny?' Hiram rushes on. The soldier starts to pull his sword out of its scabbard but one of his troop pulls his arm back shaking his head as if to say, 'don't bother'. Hiram slips on some flat, slidy stones but doesn't fall – he starts to run. I let him go – I don't want to rush; I want to look and find out what's happening.

I reach the flat ground at the side of the river and step carefully on and over smooth round rocks of all different sizes. People, women and men, are waiting to be held, dipped in the water. A breeze blows off the river as it flows – almost like the surface eddies, tiny waves, of the water have become wind. It's cooler. My friend is in the crowd somewhere. Is he safe?

Yohanan is in the water up to his knees. He's pushing his hair back across his face, out of his eyes. He's looking at the crowd watching, waiting. Oh, now he's moving quickly, splashing through the stony shallows – people move away from him like he's angry but, no, he's helping an older woman who's slipped and fallen on her knees and hands. He lifts her tenderly, walks with her further into the river and holds her as she leans back under the ripples, wetting her face and hair. She comes up, smiling, turning, gripping Yohanan's hands with both of hers - she walks back to the shore looking, somehow, straighter, stronger – a small child runs to her, and she picks them up laughing, dripping.

I'm tired now and sit back from the crowd on a bank of soft sand which fits and holds my body as I lie back to rest and watch. I doze in the warm air with wondering thoughts about why people come to the river, what happens, do they really feel like sad, bad, or hard thoughts or things they've done are washed, go away? Do they just imagine it because it's such a great river in our history? Shall I try it? I come wide awake suddenly. The noise of the crowd has changed. It's louder and then, now, still. Soldiers are moving quickly down the path, sliding, holding each other on the dusty slippy stones. Why? I look and I see in front of the red cloth, glinting metal of the soldiers is a hurrying group, women and men, smiling behind a man with thick, dark hair, tall, brown running to the river.

Yohanan is waiting. He greets, holds the man hard in his arms. Then I know it's the man Yeshua, the son of the carpenter Yosef who disappeared, he's the cousin of Yohanan. They walk, alone, holding hands, deep into the middle of the river. They seem to be arguing, in a friendly way, wrestling a bit, pushing and pulling and splashing. Yohanan holds up his hands, smiling, surrendering. Yeshua stands still, turns away from Yohanan, leans back into his arms and sinks softly, held, under the water. I look around. The crowd, the soldiers are still, like everyone holds a breath. Then Yeshua is up, even from the shore his smile is visible – Yohanan kneels in the water holding Yeshua's hands. Is that water or tears on his face?"

Alone

He was so hungry that his ribs felt broken, piercing his stomach. His abdomen curved empty, inwards. His tongue was cleft to the ridged roof of his mouth, fat and dry – unworded. Why had he walked away from the beautiful, full river? When had that been? The demand to be alone, absent from everybody and in his own emptiness had called him, again, but never before into this hazardous, starved isolation. Why now after such a time touched, filled by visceral love birthed in him, it seemed, by Yohanan with his smile, passionate holding and the prayer wrapped immersion in the cold water?

He knew what the rabbis said about being nearer to G'd in thin places – there were rules, if you're stupid you'll die. He'd heard stories from travellers about women and men living in quiet solitude often in desert but still with someone to bring a little food and, ohh, water cool in clay. But, no, not him, he'd just walked ignoring voices calling, 'wait, wait!' – his arrogant, bloody unthought out irrationality had put him in danger, again. Then, softly, the part of his mind that led him into these moments went, 'Ssssh. Stop. It will be well.' He sat, his back drinking in the cool of the shaded boulder he leant against. He clutched a small bag holding a little bread, fish, and dried fruit. Beginning to sleep in a hot hungry exhaustion still puzzled and scared, he listened, a little, for the voice that arose low down in him. He always forgot and then remembered that this was why being away and utterly alone was necessary – no other voices to listen to or things to do. Just it.

There were three dreams, torments, and monsters, so strong that each time he woke he could not move out of a physical, rending, excoriating realness. First it was hunger and bread, then domination and power and then life itself. With each torment he nearly slipped, fell, and lost what was most beloved – a pearl he would recall another time.

The first torment

It was early dawn, cold. Before sleeping he'd missed one round stone and now there was a bruised hollow in his side above his right hip, stiff. He was awakened by a brisk scratching and scrambling. He stretched and turned to the sound. A fox was hurrying with a cub nipped in her lip curled teeth. Quick she went, vivid, around and under a black rock. She came out and whimpering followed her. Four more precious cargoes filled her mouth and then she was gone, panting, into her dark shelter.

Settling, he sipped from the pooled spring by his side and, as it was dawn, chewed slowly on the last crust in his bag – it made him hungrier. He curled back into the sand, moving the stone. Sleep came without threat. Softening to rest he remembered the smell of his mum's bread and the touch of her hands sticky with yeasted dough. His mouth opened, tasting. Now deep down asleep but so strong it was like waking, a voice, words surged. 'I am who I am; I could go anywhere and take bread – not pay, I'm hungry.' Sometimes the power in him was like a high bell ringing – an alarm. 'That rock could be bread, go on, you're hungry, do it.' His hand lifted towards the rock round like a loaf, his mouth quirked in a thin smile unlike him – his tongue protruded, licking. 'Why shouldn't I? Who cares? I'm better, more needed than all the hungry. I can feed me in any way I want. Can't I? Come on – once.' Here, now, was the terror close to rending him into pieces like a sacrificer's knife wielded by a shadow, destroying his purpose for ever. Oh, he could do it, at least in a dream, but then he would look back at the trail of crumbs and know he couldn't sweep it away or follow it home like a lost child hoping for love. It would be done. G'd's back would be turned.

He slept. Between sleeping, dreaming and waking exhausted, someone came, covered in white against the sun, smiling, leaving a jar of water, bread, dates and leaf wrapped cheese. His eyes opened, his heart thumping fast and he half heard words, 'Stranger, you must eat and drink when it is permitted. You must not die. I will bring more another day.' A horse clattered away.

The second torment

He was drained by hot air and hunger despite the returning stranger's gifts. In the early morning or evening he walked, carefully, on fields of shards of rock broken by heat, water and cold. Alone, he broke his fast in the dusk. Thoughts bubbled up about his dad leaving, weaponising his tools. Where was he? Tiredness disabled his resistance to things he would avoid – he remembered strangers hung, chewed by dogs, on crosses beside busy roads. He sipped water to ease the nausea and rested his head back on his cooling rock. He managed to breathe softly, and his eyes blinked, aching, shut. A trapped eyelash spiked his pupil – he rubbed it away. He lay down, a heap of sand a pillow, his thinned cloak wrapping him. Sliding into sleep he recalled the voices of his friends, overheard, arguing, 'Why doesn't he fight? People would come – out of the hills, from their homes, all over. Armed. Fearful but ready to kill our torturers. We've had enough. We could win. We have to.'

His legs straightened and kicked as if he was standing and marching. He didn't wake. He dreamed. This time he felt the voice like a tug on his sleeve, pulling. Trembling, holding against the tug, he stood on the highest cliff imaginable of the hardest grey, slabbed rock. He saw place after place, a carpet of countries, immense fields of colour each with towers, temples and palaces – gleaming. Blocks of armies trampled, squadrons of ships on the oceans at the edges and, everywhere, people, without faces, in crowds gazing, waiting. 'Go on, give in. They want you. You can be the king of everywhere and everything. You can. You want to. Your friends, the ones who matter, the men, will love you for it. Your father can come home. Your mother will be happy. Your enemies will be ruined, their bones burned to ashes. Just decide – this is me; this is who I am.' Again, he woke, the terror of the choices offered like a rip toothed saw cutting across his belly. He knew, despite the imagined pain, that he could choose this – the world called. Justice through power or through jubilee? His heart burned as he chose.

The third torment

Now he feared that he was really about to die. Lonely. The food without company was not enough - the shared in and out of fasting had always helped. His face was filthy with dirt and grimed in sand, his beard ragged and knotted, his eyes sore in the corners. He had raw, itching patches where limbs rubbed against skin and sweat dried sand stuck. He smelt like the worst of the sick and broken beggars lost by the pools in Beth-ezda. He had left the tiny shelter of the boulder by the pool just to move and, maybe, find some purpose but all he did was stagger, slip, graze his knees, hands and stand again without direction - repeatedly. Now the sun was up. He couldn't remember what to do or where to go. He turned to escape the blaze but swayed and twisted off an angled slab and caught the brilliance like a hot punch in the eyes. He fell cutting his cheek. He cried water he couldn't spare and crawled to a shadow as a tiny bit of his mind knew he had to do. Then in an exhausted, despairing stupor he felt death nearer and there was a whisper - 'go on, ask, ask to be saved'. Falling further into flaccid collapse he sort of dreamed. He was standing on the uttermost high point of a temple, golden and pulsing through his feet. His arms stretched straight out from his shoulders, maybe wings. Sun warmed wind blew his clothes. The voice whispered again, 'go on, fall. You've said G'd is your parent, prove it, jump. You can't die, surely. Go on, I dare you. You're special. Go on'. He leaned as if launching. Asleep his hands scrabbled to grip onto the ground, he cut himself on flaked rock. He jumped awake, sweat dripped from his forehead and down into his eyes. Blinking he paused to breathe and then, in the breeze filled space, laughed, shouted, roared, laughed until he hurt to bursting. Black carrion birds clattered up from eating at the sudden noise breaking the stillness. He knew then that of course he could die and there was no magic. He turned, went to his rock and pool, found fruit and water left, again, ate a little and lay down. He slept, wrapped, for a day. He woke raptured with knowing love was with him, in him. He ate, drank and then, grinning, wrote his name in the sand and left.

Back at the river he fell into the water soaking it in through his skin, dirt, torment floating off. Now, he thought, it begins. Wading across he walked to find his friends. Yohanan was gone.

Woman at the well

She stood close up against the wall around the well, her right hand flat, palm down on its top edge as she let herself lean and rest. The damp rock was cool against the bruises on her right thigh, under her clothes, where the thrown stones had thudded as she ran. Her back also throbbed. She had paused from pulling the water to stand and gaze around her, easing. She saw a dark brown furry bee with an orange stripe sipping water from a spilt puddle; it was so attentive, its head and tiny feelers dipped down. She watched it rise and fly to a mass of blue flowers by the side of the path, tasting, and then flying, straight, away. She pulled up the water. As she poured it into a swelling skin carrier the golden hairs on her brown arms captured tiny drops shining like jewelled beads. Slowly, her leg hurting, she walked back to the copse where her friends rested, exhausted. They ate, drank, and dozed – comfortable together.

They woke refreshed, drank water. One, a younger woman, said, "tell us again how this started, what happened at that other well."

"Really, again?"

"Oh, yes, please; it reminds me, us, of why we do what we are doing – especially when others attack us."

She carefully leaned against a smooth grey barked tree, her head tipped back slightly, resting, whilst she winnowed her thoughts.

She began. "I'd hooked the bucket into the loop in the end of the rope and wound it down to the trembling circle of reflected sky at the bottom to splash and quickly, heavily, fill. I wound its weight back up, lifted it away from the well and onto the ground next to my empty jar. I moved my hands, flat, to the soft curves of my back above my hips and arched backwards, stretching. Suddenly a shadow fell across me. There was a man, someone I didn't recognise. I looked to see if he had a stick ready to hit me – I am, like some of you, Shamerim[8], and many people hated us, there as here. Also, it was midday, and I should not have been at the well – a woman's time was in the evening (just when we're cooking!). Nothing happened. Then, he said, tired sounding, 'please, may I have some water? It's been a long day.' I didn't answer – what he'd asked was startling. Surprising myself, I said, 'of course, when I've filled this jar, help yourself.'

I put the empty bucket carefully on the well wall and stepped away. He came forward, slowly, pulled water up, sat on a rock and drank so fast it dribbled from his mouth, over his chin. He splashed his face some more and laughed. I was puzzled and asked, 'Why, why would you ask me for water? Your people hate my people; you, a man, talked to me, a woman, without a sneer, a stick, or a touch I didn't want.'

I remember, so clearly, how, for a few long moments, he looked down, away from me – there was a feeling of a quiet holding of time, an extra ordinary, almost deep, stillness. It was as if he paused himself, a thought poised on a threshold that he was unsure of leaving. I could only wait. Then, sitting up, he rubbed his face, flicked away drops of water and pushed his hands through thick hair and looked directly at me. This was shocking – it wasn't a look that said, now woman, you look down or away or what have you got for me – it was a look inviting me to gaze back and not be afraid. The moment broke. Some people, women and men came up the path. They smiled at the man pointing to baskets of food they carried. Then, looking at me, some of them frowned, just as I'd expect, but they were stopped, cautioned by his raised hand, and he pointed them to a sheltered grove by a low, pink flower covered cliff. They moved away and we were uncomfortably alone. Facing me he said, 'you asked me why I asked you for water – I ask you, why didn't you pour it for me? What happened?'

I said, 'Suddenly I wasn't afraid. I chose. You'd spoken to me in a way that meant I could choose.' Smiling he said, 'Just now, before my friends came, I was going to tell you things I have never told anyone – I hesitated because they didn't understand why I should talk with you, a Shamerim. I've seen you before, heard about you from gossiping men in the market as you walked by, and heard what they call you. I know you are not a free born woman so you can't choose to marry. I know about the five husbands you have had and lost and the one you live with, freed but not free born. I can only guess the sadness and the hurt.'

I was angry at his cheek, talking about me, my life – I said, anger flaring, 'what has this to do with you? It's not your business – how dare you.'

He held his hands out in front of him, palms downwards, suggesting apology and calm. 'Oh, I know, sorry, but my time here is short, and I have to seek out helpers and people who, maybe, think differently or who might be prepared to try. When I saw you, what did I see? – a woman pulling up water when she shouldn't; a woman telling a man to wait his turn for water; a woman, by herself, who doesn't hide her face or pretend to look after or do what a man wants; a woman who didn't flinch or run away – a Shamerim, not afraid. You see? Sometimes there are people I can just speak to or ask – it happens. Shall I say more?'

I had to grip the edge of the well in case I fell. I had never been spoken with like this. 'Yes, please.' He walked towards me holding the bucket with cold water still in it. 'Drink.' I scooped a handful, spilling, swallowed – glad of its flow in my dry, gripped throat. 'Soon you will need more in the heat of the day. This well has been here for 1,000 years and never run dry – you can always drink. There is another well, invisible, that also never runs dry – it is in you, in me, in everyone if they choose to look. It rises and falls, filling with something like cool clear water, ebbing and flowing. I know it is very dangerous to say this. It means that everyone can know what is in the middle of us all, not outside us hidden behind a screen or a curtain or wrapped up in too many words. It means, if we want, that we can remake this world now. This is what I bring to say and ask you if you can also say. These are not old, tired words but are like the first drink of the day. Think for a moment and then, if you can, go, go bring your husband, your family and anybody else who will come to see me.'

I paused, waiting for my heart to slow so I could breathe, then turned, ran, ran to the centre of the town."

The young woman gripped the hand of the man next to her as the shock of the day and people's hatred and the repeat of the story turned to tears and relief. Photini[9], the storyteller, was still, resting her leg.

Later, quietly, they began to walk to the next town. Photini didn't know then that, one day, there would be another well where she would die.

8 For the rabbi, Yeshua, to choose a Shamerim woman to talk with would have been, and still is, for some, shocking. The Samaritans, Shamerim or Shomeronim (Hebrew for 'to conserve') is an ancient community with a story more than 2,500 years old. Today just a few hundred survive after millennia of persecution and absorption. They trace their narrative back to the expulsion of the Judean (Jewish) population by the Assyrians in 701 BCE – they remained. On the return of descendants of the Judean exiles from Babylonia 200 years later the people who were to become the Shamerim refused to accept new religious texts and interpretations. They held to their belief that only the first five books of the bible have authority and that Moses is the only prophet. The returning Judeans, equally, refused to work or collaborate with the Shamerim. There was also a fundamental dispute over the site of the original 'holy places of Israel' – for the Judeans it was the Temple Mount of Moriah' in Jerusalem; for the Shamerim it was Mount Gerizim, and rival temples were built. Because of theses deep theological disputes the Shamerim, particularly, became loathed. For more information go to: https://en.wikipedia.org/wiki/Samaritans

9 Photini was a famous advocate and proselytiser. Her name means 'enlightened one'. She travelled and spoke throughout Samaria with her sisters and other family members. She was murdered by being thrown into a dry well after she had gone to Rome and tried to convert Nero and members of his family. In Eastern orthodox churches she is a saint. Misogynistic religious commentary describes her as a rescued or forgiven 'sinner' – this is rebutted at: https://tinyurl.com/2wbb9bza

Miryam of Magdala

Fish hung spiked on racks at the front of the house. They were fresh caught and sunshine sparkled silver and rainbow on their scales – like tiny reflections of the lake. The air smelt of fish and of water on rocks – just drying. Nets were also hanging, rippling in the breeze from the water.

A man called Baruch was passing.

Baruch speaks:

"As I walk up the worn path towards the houses near the lake a door crashes and then there's running and shouting. I know this family; I pass their house every day – I buy fish from them. The shouting sounds like Miryam. I wonder what has driven that quiet, peaceful woman to such fury. 'I will not marry him!' I see the door, blue, swing open, again, and slam back. Her father is after her, his fists bony and hard, the knuckles clenched white – 'you will do as I tell you. You do not have any choice in this at all! You are just a woman'.

Well, I have never seen a woman look at a man with such disgust, especially a daughter at her father. They both notice me standing on the path. Miryam nods at me and walks with fast angry steps away towards the edge of the lake. She sits. Her dad turns like he has been beaten and hurt and goes back to the house – he says nothing to me. I walk on."

Miryam walked along the shore careful not to get soaking feet. She listened to the tiny gentle waves breaking softly – this always helped. "I am different – I don't want to be married, not yet anyway. I'm not poor that I need another man, after Papa, to feed me. I know I make him so angry – he doesn't mean to, but he treats me like a sheep he can't afford or bear to lose - there has to be more." She's been speaking her thoughts as she walked, getting louder again. She heard soft footsteps close to her, turned, felt a hand touch her shoulder, pull away quick and a man's voice say, "what more do you want?" She looked at him, shocked. He'd just come to her, a woman, and asked a question. She might be unclean, having her period – how would he know? They could both be in trouble. The sun caught her sharp in the eyes, she couldn't see – she had a moment to step back, cover her face, make space in case the man was a danger. What did he want? They always want something and, whatever it is, they usually want you to do it for them. He was tall, tired and smiling at the same time. He put his hands up in front of him, "I'm sorry, I shouldn't have touched you". Again, what was happening – men don't usually say sorry. She saw there was a group of women and men further away, some sitting on the ground, others standing, watching –were they with him?

"You don't have to answer – I heard your plea for more and wondered what you meant. I forget sometimes, I'm so used to talking like this to my friends over there that I do it with strangers without thinking. We're about to eat and rest – would you like to join us?" He walked away, hesitated. She didn't know what, but something tugged her, had her interested, stirred her up. She walked quietly with the man. The women, some lying down with their heads in another's lap, were sitting together. Nearby the men, talking but not shouting – listening. Food and drink were being passed between them – sharing, not the men first. She settled, suddenly shy.

The man had stopped and sat at the edge of the group – one of the men had taken him food. After a little while he stood and came to the rough circle of his friends, sitting now on sand and rocks. Miryam saw them all turn their attention to him, quiet – there was an odd feeling of warmth, even love. She heard a woman nearby say, softly – "will he tell us a story now?" He looked around and began, "The kingdom of heaven is like when a person takes the tiniest of all the seeds, a mustard seed, a seed so small that, if I had one on my fingertip you would not be able to see it. The person puts the seed in the ground and soon, it begins to grow. The shrub grows up so big that it looks like a little tree. Birds come and make nests in it." He stopped, looked around and drank. Nobody spoke. Then quietly, the woman who spoke before, looking at Miryam, said, "He never ever tells you what a story means. He just lets it work."

Miryam cried, softly, a single tear moved slowly, tickling slightly, down the side of her nose by her cheek. She dared not move in case she lost, somehow spilled, the feeling she had – like the seed was in her and, at the same time, she's a safe nesting bird come home as she might also be a nest. He smiled at her. The woman moved a little closer to her.

A while later, feeling calm, strong, and nervous all mixed up she leaves them waiting. She would tell her father she was going to travel with these new people.

A father's sick child

Once there was a child, a girl. Her dad was rich – he had lots of money and had all of the things, clothes and food that they could ever want. His name was Jairus. I wonder what his daughter was called.

He was often very busy and, even though he had lots of men to do the work he wanted in fields, orchards, and workshops (this was how he made his money) and many women to cook and clean the house and to look after his children, he was still busy. He didn't see his daughter as much as she wanted or needed. She missed him and he didn't listen to his thoughts about missing her – he thought his work was more important.

One day, he woke up, got out of bed and washed his face and hands with fresh cold water put in a bowl by one of the women who had been up very early in the morning.

He began to eat breakfast – soft warm bread, honey and fruit that had been brought to his room.

He was startled when, without knocking or asking permission, one of the women ran into his room – "sir, sir your daughter, your daughter, she is very ill. Come, come now." He was about to shout at the woman about rushing in but stopped himself when her words caught up with him. He rushed to where his daughter slept. She still looked asleep but, really, she was ill and could not be woken. He tried to wake her, calling her name, holding her hand. Her skin was wet and sweaty. Her eyes were closed.

Suddenly, he felt something that he had never, ever felt before – he was afraid, scared that he might lose something, someone very precious to him. He thought she might die.

Then, he remembered that he had heard of a man in town, a special teacher who told stories and did amazing things – helping people, anybody, who was in trouble or sick. Jairus ran out of his house away from his daughter to find the man – to ask for help.

Would he come to help Jairus, a rich man? Would he want to be paid lots of money? He remembered as he ran that the man's name was Yeshua – not a rich man like him but someone who made things out of wood, a carpenter. Rushing, running, breathing very fast Jairus saw a crowd in the market and there, there was a man talking to them and they were listening and not arguing. It must be him he thought. He ran to the crowd and pushed his way in shouting, "Help me, help me." The man turned and looked at him and quietly asked, "What's the matter?" "My daughter, she's sick, she might already be dead. Please, please come." He grabbed hold of the cloth of the sleeve of the man's gown – a man next to Yeshua went to push Jairus away but Yeshua just held up his hand and walked into the crowd with Jairus who still held onto him. He paused and looked around everybody and said, "sorry, I'll come back soon."

He walked fast with Jairus but, in a funny way, even though he walked fast, Jairus felt that he was calm and still – a bit like a deep pool of water that wind is rustling on the surface.

They came to the house and went straight to the girl's room. She had not woken or moved. The room felt quiet, like it was waiting. Was she breathing? Yeshua sat on a small wooden stool by the bed – it was like something he might have made. He held her hand and stroked her head. After a few moments she opened her eyes. Yeshua turned to her dad and said, "feed her, she is ravenous. Give her fruits with thick hides, food with weight to keep her here."[10]. Jairus ran to the kitchen and asked one of the women there for help – he didn't know where food was kept. He came back to the bedroom with a clay cup of cool water and a plate of sweet melon, pomegranate, peeled dates all soft green and pink - all chopped and shining fresh. She ate some – her eyes lighting with the sweetness and juice and taste. Jairus cried softly. The other people in the house who loved and cared for her crowded around the door inside and outside the room also cried. Yeshua touched Jairus gently on the shoulder, smiled and quietly said goodbye.

10 This is two lines from an exquisite poem, *Jairus*, by Michael Symmons Roberts: https://poetryarchive.org/poem/jairus/ I heard it in the worship at a national ecumenical conference of church children's workers. The priest for the session, Peter Privett, had brought a huge platter of fruits and a large knife!

The woman who bled

Once there was a woman called Beronike[11]

Beronike speaks:

"I don't know what to do. We have no more money for medicine, and I am still bleeding – we can't sell any more animals and the tax has to be paid. The priests are no good, they won't help – they tell my husband to pray more and tell me, again, that I'm unclean and to come back in 40 days and be purified. What do they know? I'd like them to bleed like this and get no help. Useless, useless men. I can't look after my children properly and my husband is so worried and worn out. I need to rest now."

After several hours hot and uncomfortable sleep, she wakes to hear excited, loud voices outside the house. She gets up slowly, cleans herself with a wet cloth and rinsing it leaves it to soak in a bucket with a round, close fitting wooden lid. Pulling a shawl around her shoulders she goes outside. There's a crowd of her neighbours around a group of women and men who are walking quickly down the street. They look tired – one of them especially so. She asks a friend – "what's happening?" The woman says, "It's that man who everybody is talking about, the son of Miryam in Naz'-a -reth, the storyteller, rabbi. They say he's a messiah but, I don't know, he looks like any grubby shepherd to me. They're going to the house of Jairus, you know the synagogue leader, his daughter is sick, maybe dying. Huh, what can this man do?" Beronike, the woman who is bleeding, feels a sudden excitement. She's heard this man helps people in all sorts of trouble – can make people better. She walks forwards, staggering a little, weak, pushing into the crowd as the man goes by. She reaches out, hoping, grasps his gown as he passes – just for a moment. He turns, angrily, "who touched me? I'm too tired for this." She looks at him shocked at his sudden flare of unkindness – it's not what she expected, hoped for. She ducks her head down, trembling and weak, ashamed but says, "it was me; I need your help and don't know what to do. I'm embarrassed to ask but I can't stop bleeding and I have children I can't look after enough". The man looks at her, pauses, breathes, knowing the rule she has broken, and grasps her hands. People around are shocked – "she's unclean!" He says, "Oh, I am so sorry – I am weary too but that's no reason to snap at you when you had hope. Here, walk with me, let me help you along until you can sit on that wall over there." His arm across her shoulder was warm, comforting, reassuring. Her hope rose more.

11 Beronike is the Greek version of the name Veronica. Veronica is the name of the woman who is credited with wiping the face of the man Yeshua and thus making the shroud of Turin. It is a sometimes controversial element in the Stations of the Cross walked in churches at Easter.

The nameless woman

A woman is sitting on a stool her husband uses for cutting, shearing the wool from the sheep, her back warm against the wall of their small house. She's feeding their baby – tiny and hungry, one of its hands gripping her finger tight like a branch. The woman, we don't know her name, is drifting and thinking about the man Yeshua and his friends – what he's been saying, who they've been helping and, sometimes, how difficult and dangerous he could be. She'd heard whispers about Yeshua and women - no, not like that but that they, too, walked and worked with him and helped their group live. Oooeee," she thought, "the priests won't like that one bit. They must hate him."

She's had no time to go and hear him talk – she's just too busy being with and looking after their children – 10, 7, 3 years and 3 months old. So, today, she's excited. Yeshua and his friends are going to be walking through her village – she hopes they come near so she can see.

Goats run down the street – the lead animal's bell clanging and rattling side to side with a brassy, hard sound – like a warning bell. People come out of their houses – some with baskets of bread and fruit, others putting jugs of water on the ground with clay cups outside their doors all ready to share. The woman stands, with her baby wrapped, carefully, with a stripy cloth, safe on her front. She's standing with some friends and neighbours, chatting and smiling. Her other children are running, chasing, shouting and laughing with their friends – in and out of houses, up and down the road, in the fields. There are sharp curved winged birds diving and swooping low over buildings, catching flies, screeching.

A dusty, smiling crowd of women and men come through a gap in a rock wall by the orchard and turn into the road towards where the woman stands. As they get closer one of her friends says to her, "hey, isn't the man at the front that carpenter who made your stool? Or was it his dad – the one who disappeared?" The woman looks – it is him, it's the man Yeshua. She feels funny. She'd been excited about seeing, meeting, listening to this man who was saying such amazing things thinking he was big, important, and now she knows him; she has sat on a stool he'd made that her husband used amongst the sheep.

Everybody in the street moves towards the walkers offering food and drink. It's a dusty, swirling, friendly crowd. She feels suddenly shy. One of the walkers sees her, standing a little back – she comes to her, smiling, and touches her arm. "Hello, I'm Miryam. I'm from Magdala." The woman smiles back, says her name and strokes her baby's head. "That man, Yeshua, he made my husband's shearing stool – I feed my baby sitting on it." Miryam smiles; somehow the woman feels warm and safe with this stranger. "Oh, you too – we keep meeting people who Yeshua or his dad has made things for." The woman looks at Miryam. - her hair is pulled back from her face, her arms bare and dark brown. She smells of warm sweat and deep musky oil. The woman asks, "why do you walk with him – are you the wife or servant of him or one of the men?" Miryam stops smiling and looks at the woman and then laughs gently – "no, no – I am here because he is my friend and Rabbi, and we are close. I have found out things from him about being a woman and my religion that I did not think were possible. You know, when he talks about what the scrolls say, everything changes. It's like he reminds us of what G'd wants us to be and do. Sometimes he makes my head spin." Miryam looks around and holds the woman's arm – "some of the men here don't always like or understand what he says to or about women, and he has had to learn a lot too, but I know when he talks about heaven on earth, it includes me. Come, come say hello."

Angry men, children and two more stories

One day in the small woods outside a little but busy town, the man called Yeshua was sitting under a tree, enjoying its shade. The sun was hot, and the ground was dusty. He was thirsty. He had been talking and listening to lots of people who were hungry for what he said and for stories he told. He felt a bit pulled about and jangled and just wanted a bit of time away from people, maybe a short nap.

He had a special group of friends who travelled with him wherever he went. They helped him and tried to learn things from him. Today they knew he was tired and left him alone.

As he was resting, leaning against the tree he heard angry voices. He thought, "That's my friends – what's going on?" He slowly stood up, holding onto the rough bark of the tree to help him. He got a splinter in the palm of his hand and stopped to carefully pull it out; he licked his hand to clean it. Then, just a little way down the stony slope he found his friends standing in a group looking angry and talking loudly and pointing at some children and grownups – probably mums and dads. He heard the words, "You can't come, he's resting, go away." He stepped up close to the small crowd and said, "Stop this. What's happening?" One of his friends turned to him and said, "You were resting, you're tired and these people wanted to bring their children to see you so you could talk to them. They tried to bring their children close to you earlier today, but the crowd was too big. We told them, go away, and come on another day."

Yeshua looked hard at his friends, shook his head, sighed a big breath in and out and said in a voice that was tired and upset, "Thank you for wanting me to rest but you must never, ever turn children away. They must always come to me when they want or need to. You see, they know things that many of you have forgotten. If they want to come to see me, I think it's because, somehow, they know they are closer to G'd, to a sort of love that is like the love of their mums and dads but also a bit different and just theirs. They don't think it – they just know it; sometimes I wish you all knew things as brilliantly clear as a child!" The friends were very surprised, even shocked, and very embarrassed. They looked at the children and parents and said, "come, come now, we're sorry." Yeshua knelt down and the children crowded around, talking, laughing, and just being close. He touched each child gently on the head, the arm or shoulders - saying a soft prayer or blessing with each touch. A child said, "please, tell us a story" and he sat down asking everyone, children, parents and his friends to sit in a circle around him in the sheltered glade of trees where he had rested earlier.

He began, "Who would like to hear a puzzle? Who's clever enough to get a puzzle right even if there are lots of different answers?" The children sat up really straight and waved their hands like flower heads in a quick breeze or just called out "me, me". Adults also leaned in, eager, a bit excited.

"OK. Excellent. I was cross just now – cross with my friends and I'm sorry if our loud voices scared you. I think I was also cross with me – I am very, very impatient sometimes when grownups just won't understand what I'm saying – again and again they don't seem to get it. It might be that I don't tell a story or a puzzle right or enough times. So, I'm going to try another time with a story and puzzle some of you will have heard before – keep your ears and your heart open to what it might say or mean to you. Are you ready? Here we go.

A little seed

One day a man was walking slowly up and down a field. He, his family, and friends had worked hard moving rocks and stones and breaking lumps of hard sun-dried earth. Some of his family and friends waited now at the side of the field with jugs of precious water balanced on the ground ready to help him when he asked. In his left hand was a white cloth bag that he held, softly, cupped, so as not to spill what was in it. He licked a finger on his right hand and dipped it in the bag - it came out with several little round seeds stuck to it. He was careful, if he dropped one he might lose it. Folding the finger with the seeds into the palm of his hand, he gently put the bag down. Kneeling on the warm ground he poked a little hole in the earth with a finger and, oh so carefully, picked up and dropped a seed into the hole and covered it with loose soil, patting it flat. From a small brown bag hung over his shoulder he took out a little blade of dried yellow straw and pushed it into the ground next to where he'd planted the seed - his helpers with water would know where to slowly trickle it to help the seed swell, feed and grow. He did this more than 100 times until the little field was decorated with yellow stalks like tiny trees. Every day he, and his helpers, would come and water - even when the first bright green leaves poked out like hands reaching upwards. Once the plants were strong he stopped going every day and left the field of black mustard to grow until each plant was more than twice as tall as he was. Before it was time to harvest the seeds and feed the leaves and stalks to sheep, goats and camels there were swirls of birds over the field who rested and nested, safe. All this made the man happy."

Yeshua, the storyteller, stopped and looked around. "Now, here's the puzzle question - I wonder, what do you think the story might tell us about making heaven on earth?" There was a hush and there were frowns of thinking on the faces of people of all ages. Was it too hard a puzzle?

A brown bird with a speckled front, flicking its wings flew above everyone's heads into the shade of a tree in the glade and sang a loud rippling song, unafraid.

A small child, maybe four years old, said, "Well, it's like if we keep planting seeds there will be enough food for everybody, even the birds." Another child, maybe nine years old, said, "this is very complicated. I think the seed is a bit like something in each of us, each other, which we have to look after very carefully so it can grow. Then we can become like a home for each other." A woman said, "G'd, love has no hands so needs help and we can be that help, the hands. Everybody helped the man planting and growing. It wasn't just him." A man said, "Everybody's hands doing the work, making it happen? What about a Roman with a whip?" The storyteller asked, "What does anybody else wonder or think?"

Later, after sharing food and drink, everybody sat, rested and ready to hear more. Yeshua thought he could at least give them one more story though his friends, women and men, looked at him, carefully, with worried eyes. He noticed their worry but said, "I don't know how long I have here so I must do what I can and when." His friends touched by sadness and fear, flinched.

Carefully moving a shiny black and green beetle from the trunk of the tree behind him, he leaned on a blanket bunched against the crinkled rough and mossy bark.

After looking around at each face and smiling, he said, "now, here's a story that I'm in for a little bit. It started when someone asked me a question to try and trick me and get me into trouble, maybe arrested. But, before I say more, has anyone heard the word rachamim[12]? It doesn't matter if you haven't." A mother, holding her new baby, smiled, nodded and, answering, spoke shyly – 'it's like the ache I feel holding Rachel here, you can call it love but it's, well, it's like something in my arms, my muscles, in my middle, my womb even, that wants to protect her from any hurt and, then, if I see somebody else hurting, the same feeling somehow reaches out to, wants to enfold them.' He smiled, "yes, that's it. This story is a bit about rachamim."

A kind Shamerim

'One day I was standing in the Temple talking with friends, old and new. A man, he worked for the priests in the Temple, came up to me, interrupted and said, in a loud, important voice so everybody nearby could hear, 'what do you think is the most important of the commands we're told to live by?' I smiled at him - he was hoping I would say something wrong or dangerous or stupid that he could tell his priest bosses so that they could stop me telling stories or talking. They loved rules but also hoped I'd break them. I stood still and thought - so long that he began to fidget and look nervous in the small cluster of people gathered around him and me. Finally, I said, 'Well, in a way there are two that are almost equal but not quite - love G'd with your heart and mind and love your neighbour like you would love yourself. Sometimes the second one is harder.' The man from the Temple, he was a reader of books and very clever, said, 'you are right but just one more question - who is your neighbour?' I smiled, this was another trick so, again, I stood and thought and began to wonder if there was a story I could tell. There was – I remembered something I had heard in a village we walked through. I sat and invited everybody else also to sit, equal. I said to the man, 'my answer is a story - will you listen?' He nodded. I began.

'A man was lying on sharp stones by the side of a road in a rocky valley. Alone. He was very still, blood had trickled, dried, across his forehead and down his cheek. He was the most frightened anyone could be. Supposing birds came to peck him? What about wild dogs? He cried - tears stinging in a cut. Supposing nobody came, he'd never see his children, Rebecca and Samuel, again - they wouldn't know where he was. What would his wife, Adira, do? He stretched his legs, turned over and crawled. He looked like a rock moving slowly as he dragged himself to the thin shade under a burned dead tree. He hadn't seen the masked face staring over a boulder or the wave to the other man, hiding behind a thorny bush, who threw the rock that knocked him to the ground. He'd felt their hands pulling, knives cutting, ripping his bag from his shoulder - heard them laugh when they found his purse, food and wine. He'd smelt them - wood smoke, sweat and urine. He'd heard them running away, leaving him in the rippling, hot silence. Would anybody come?

A mum, a dad and their child, a girl, came to the mouth of the same rocky valley. She wore a russet skirt and blouse, he was wearing a white gown and a round white cap, their daughter was dressed in brown baggy trousers and an old white shirt of her dad's. The dad walked whilst the mum and the daughter took it in turns to ride on their mule, soft and grey, plodding, swaying with bags tied, swinging, to a saddle. This was a country where most people hated them. They were from a tribe called Shamerim[13] but here, well, mainly they were called scum, defilers. The mother was riding, nodding, almost asleep. The daughter was skipping and running ahead just a little. Her dad kept watch on her and on the valley slopes - he kept his hand on a short stabbing sword.

Turning a curve in the valley and out of sight for a moment, the girl stopped, stared and yelled, 'Abba, Abba!' He ran and his wife, Esther, jumped, almost fell from the mule and then stood firm, holding the animal's lead, stroking its thick strong, bristly neck, calming.

He found the child kneeling on rocks next to a ragged heap of clothing. 'It's a man and his head is broken'. He stroked his daughter's thick dark hair, crouched beside her. He saw the blood, still red but matting. He said, 'run, go tell mumma to bring the mule and everything. Be careful, don't trip.' He waited, now sitting, whispering, 'don't worry now - we'll help you, don't worry.' The man moaned and moved a little as if he'd heard.

The father, let's call him Abel, hadn't had a moment to feel fear but now, in the pause, he did, his breathing quick and tight high in his chest. His family was strung out, separate, out of sight. Who had hurt this man, were they still near, watching? He gently touched the man on the shoulder and lightly gripped. The hurt man feeling a hand on him turned and, seeing the Shamerim cap[14], whimpered and tried to haul himself away - 'you are going to kill me; you're Shamerim and I'm Jew.' Abel sighed, sad, shook his head, 'No, I'm going to help you.'

'Why,' the hurt man said, 'the others didn't, and they weren't like you?' Before he could ask, what others? Esther came quick, breathless and anxious with the mule rattling hooves on rocks. The girl, Sarah, dark eyes bright with rivulets of tears in dusty dirt on her cheeks, was both scared and excited. Abel kept whispering soft reassurance, 'we're here, we'll help, let's clean you, here sip some water' as he, so carefully, aided the hurt man, still fear full, to sit up and settle back against the meagre tree. With a smile to Abel who nodded back, Esther began to clean the man's face and ease the blood dried in his hair - now they could see his wound was not so bad. Her fingers moved a wet cloth lightly as if cleaning a baby - dabbing so as not to hurt or alarm. Offering him a clean cloth she held a bottle of water and poured as he, shaking, cleaned his hands. Abel saw how soiled with dirt and fear the man's clothes were and pulled a fresh gown from a bag - Esther and Miriam turned away whilst Abel persuaded and helped the man to undress and dress crouched low on rocks. The filthy gown was wrapped for washing later.

'Will you leave me here?' Esther, Sarah and Abel all smiled. Abel spoke, 'no of course not. In a little while we will take you somewhere to rest and be well. But, before that, share some food with us and tell us what has happened and who were the others who left you.' Eating bread, dates and cheese he told what he remembered. After he had been hurt and robbed, a man, like a soldier or guard, had looked at him, leaning in, about to help but a voice from further away had shouted, 'stop, don't touch him, we can't do anything, come now' and then he was alone, again. The hurt man said, 'where will you take me? I have no money.' Looking first at Esther, Abel said, 'just past the exit of this valley is a village and there is a Khan there where we will leave you. We will leave money for the Khan and for you - it is our gift to help you get well and back to your home. Come, let's help you onto our mule and get going before dark.' Carefully, gently Esther and Abel pushed, pulled and lifted the man onto the blanketed mule while Sarah held the reins, stroked the animal's head and softly whispered thankyou to it for being so strong. They began walking with the hurt man on the mule leaning forward resting his head.'

The storyteller looked around at everybody, 'oh, before I ask you some puzzles there's one more thing to tell.' The Temple worker, the one who asked the questions, jumped up suddenly when I finished. He looked very uncomfortable, frightened. 'How did you know? I couldn't help it - I couldn't do my job for seven days if I'd helped him!' Then he ran away. After that there were people sitting with me with eyes shining with tears, others looked down, quiet. I stood, smiled and left with my friends.'

Now a couple of puzzles. What would you do if a Shamerim came to help you? What would you do if you found a Shamerim family injured, robbed? Supposing it was a Temple worker, a priest or a robber you found? Supposing it was a Roman who might die? Is rachamim for everybody?'

There was a pause, it was quiet. Somehow the green and black beetle had climbed from the tree and was walking like a living jewel down his arm. A child pointed and laughed, 'look!' The storyteller cupped it in his hands and let it walk off, tickling, under fallen leaves amongst roots curving into the ground at the bottom of the tree. The little crowd began to quietly chat and pass round more food and drink. Yeshua noticed his friends were talking with and listening to children. He was glad of some water and some bread and dried fish that a child brought to him, proudly.

12 *'Rachamim' the Hebrew word for compassion is rooted in the word 'rechem' meaning womb. For more detail see: https://tinyurl.com/w8v2dufk*

13 *The choice by the rabbi of Shamerim, Samaritans, as central characters for this parable is eye wateringly provocative. The story of the 'Good Samaritan' is told again and again in schools and churches as a simplistic moral fable that, in its telling, directs listeners to one particular meaning. It is, however, much more complex and dangerous. Today you might, perhaps, entitle the story the 'Good Palestinian'.*

14 *A round white peakless cap.*

Death in custody: a mother and cousin hear the news.

The mother. In the garden the woman, Elizabeth, was hoeing weeds from between rows of beans that would be dried for food for later in the year. The hoe struck against stones under the surface – newly risen from deeper down – and she remembered the same sound, years before, when Yohanan was unborn and he'd leapt inside her when Miryam, her cousin, had come close. Mmmm....she said to herself, odd that I should recall that now. She straightened up and stretched her back – she ached from bending and pushing. In the late afternoon quiet she heard somebody running and looked to the wall of broken rocks at the side of the garden along the edge of the path. It was Amos, her neighbour, hurrying and tripping. He came to the low, old gate. He was carrying a cloak, brown and torn at the edge, dragging the ground, flapping. He saw her, stopped, and then, looking like he wanted, at the same time, to run away, stepped towards her. She saw his face, dusty, muddy trickles from his eyes like tiny streams or shapes of river. Her heart beat hard; she felt it in her throat. He looked at Elizabeth as if it was the hardest thing he had ever done. He said, "It's Yohanan. He's dead. Herod killed him. Here, here is his cloak." She grasped it to her, seeing the dark stains spoiling the soft cloth. Her legs couldn't hold her, and she fell forwards onto the ground her head hitting one of the stones. She bled and was utterly silent for a moment and then a howl came from her wide, open mouth and she rolled in the soil, crushing plants, holding her belly, remembering the baby inside her. Amos ran, ran to get help.

The cousin. The tiny waves on the lake are sparkling, shimmering – sequinned. This light shines in the tears that trickle from the man's eyes, over his cheeks and into his beard. He rubs them away as they itch. The man, who is called Yeshua, shakes his head as if to get thoughts sorted or out of his mind. To himself he says, "Yohanan is dead. That mamzer, murdering king killed him and gave his head as a gift, a gift! – to a woman not his wife. My cousin, the man who poured water from the river Jordan over my head with a prayer and a blessing that was so powerful and kind. The man who helped me get to now." He looks out over the sides of the strong, wooden fishing boat, it rocks a little. The quiet and peace out on the lake are like medicine or someone gently stroking his head. "I'm alone again – I know G'd is always here (he touches his chest) but always, always people special or close to me leave, die or I have to leave them. This sadness it's so big – I see more of it coming and I can't stop it - people who are with me now will leave me, let me down when I need them most. Oh, I need this quiet just a little more."

A big picnic, and what is a miracle?

In a small village by a road between two towns, near a lake with lots of fish, nothing much happened except normal day to day things – looking after sheep and goats, planting, harvesting and picking, playing, eating, cooking, singing, building, loving, baking, arguing, hugging, learning, sleeping, dreaming and much more.

On the day of our story, it is very hot. The sun is bright in the sky and there are scents in the air of the village of cooking herbs, of sun warmed leaves and flowers. Something different is happening. As people talk to their neighbours, go to a shared well for water or work in orchards or fields, they say things like, "Have you heard? That Rabbi is coming, the young man, the one who tells stories and turns things, ideas, upside down, breaks rules and does amazing things. He is going to be on the hillside by the lake to talk to anybody who wants to listen. He came past the village in the early morning with his friends – women and men they say. Well, some people who saw him say he looked tired, others that he looked strong, others still that he looked sad and hopeful at the same time. Will you go?"

A child called Sara hears all the talk and buzz. Sometimes it stops people doing their jobs. Sara is only small and is jealous that some of her friends are going. She knows that her mum is too busy, and her dad has a new fold for sheep to finish before night comes. She doesn't know what to do. She loves stories and wants to be with everyone else she knows, doesn't want to be left out. She knows there will be trouble, but she doesn't want to be told no so when her mum is not in the house, she grabs a basket and quickly puts some bread and some dried fish into it; she also takes a clay bottle of water. She runs out and joins the crowd of people leaving her village. They all know her, so no one asks if she has permission. They walk on the road alongside the lake and then onto a stony track up the hill under trees with leaves silvery grey on one side and green on the other. Sara sees the man standing a little way up the hill; some people are close to him – probably the friends who are always with him. Sara and some friends sit in the shade of a tree and have a drink – they are careful with the water as the day is hot and they will be thirsty as well as hungry by lunch time.

The man, Yeshua, begins to speak. There is a hush as people listen carefully – everyone is still as they all want to hear. It is like nothing that Sara has heard before. The man tells stories and says things that are funny, exciting and a bit scary. He says that the poorest people can be closest to G'd, to love, and that they are powerful. He talks about a new way of life, about heaven being on earth now – Sara sees the man's hands sort of pull downwards as if bringing heaven here. An hour or two pass quickly and, before anyone realises, it's time to stretch and to eat. Listening, being still, concentrating is quite hard work. Yeshua stops talking and takes a break. Suddenly, Sara notices people start to getting fidgety – they are hungry. People start to get grumpy – there are voices saying, "what do you mean there's no food? I didn't bring any. They should have brought some. Why aren't there any stalls? It's no good dragging folks out here miles from home or a market and not laying on food and drink. Call this heaven!" Sara looks at her little basket with its few fish and a little bread. It's all she's got – it was all the spare food in the house and she's hungry too, but she can't just eat it all herself without sharing it – can she? Before she even realises what she's doing she stands up, holds the basket tightly in front of her and walks slowly, step by step through the crowd towards the man who has been speaking. She doesn't look at anybody – not even her friends who call out and ask where she's going.

Yeshua is surrounded by his friends – the women are seated, quietly, resting, but some of the men, big blokes, are standing with their backs to the crowd. Sara keeps going. She has to push a bit through the squash of people near Yeshua. Some of the men, hungry too and a bit cross as well, tell her to stop it and go away but one, a big smiling, sunny faced man like a fisherman from her village, with big hands and skin made deep brown from sunshine, salt and water, puts a gentle hand on her shoulder. Sara says, "I have this to share if it helps?" The man smiles, turns to Yeshua and says something she can't hear. Yeshua turns and looks at her but also sort of into her (it feels funny); he looks at the food. In the basket and in what the child has done Yeshua sees something, a solution to their problem and also some danger. To share breaks the food rules but if a child shows the way then…? Sara sees Yeshua decide. Straightaway he tells everyone standing to sit down; the sea of people sinks and settles again on the hillside. No more shoving and arguing – someone, a child has done something. Yeshua tells them what Sara has done and holds up the basket. There are nods, smiles, sighs and some worried looks. Yeshua breaks the bread and fish into small pieces, gives some to Sara and then starts to share it, giving some first to children and women nearest to him and then to men. Sara sees other people starting to share the little pieces of food that they have brought with them. It looks like a wave of movement through the crowd as people share, laugh, eat, thank each other, and give to those without anything or too nervous to ask. Sara hears someone say, "Is this what he means about heaven being here, now?" Yeshua also hears it and smiles at Sara. The kindness of a thought less child has brought a feast. She is glad she stood up and then remembers she has to go home soon. What will she say to her mum and dad? What will they say to her?

The mother

She knew she shouldn't go near the house, she could hear the laughter, the joy of a meal with friends after busy days but she didn't have time to wait for the man to come out - when...to go home?....to use the bushes for a toilet? She wasn't like them, not a Jew. She was Greek, different Gods, to them just a goyim[15].

Thick drops of rain bounced off the wind-blown flapping leaves of the fig tree and splashed like tiny crowns in the dry dust. The woman sheltered, her hair clinging to and dripping down her face and onto the shoulders of her dress. She swore to herself, 'damn, I'm a soggy mess'. She'd left her daughter asleep, finally. Her husband was in with the animals - he had to work early in the morning; soldiers had grabbed and ordered him to carry their packs and tools. His mother was sitting with the child who was sick, and they didn't know why and had no more money to pay the apothecary[16]. She had heard of this man who, somehow, helped people get better or get help. She was scared, desperate - her youngest child, she'd only had two, had died falling from a wall as she ran along its top.

She decided. She walked out into the rain and to the door, ajar to let cool air flow through. Pausing, her heart so fast and thumping she was sure it could be heard - an alarm beating out for help. Pulling the door by a rope handle she stepped in. Nothing happened then a big man saw her, laughed – "look what the rain washed in." Ignoring him and the ridiculing smiles she walked close to the table and held the back of a chair where a woman, eating, sat. She saw the man, gazed at him – "I am sorry, but I need your help, my child is sick, and I thought, hoped, you might come."

He put down his cup and slapped his hands on the tabletop, "why should I help you foreigner? What have you to do with me?" The woman in the chair stiffened. The knuckles on the mother's hand hardened until you could see the outline of the bone - hard, punching. "Why?

Because," as she saw a skinny animal creep away, tail down, "even the dogs under your table get scraps to eat." The woman in the chair turned and held the mother's hand and then, thin lipped, flamed her fury past all the other guests, who ducked, towards the man at the end.

The only sounds were the rain and the dog crunching a bone. Then, after a long minute, the man reached for an empty cup, filled it with warming wine, walked to the mother and gave it to her. She drank, quickly and gladly. "I am sorry. I was as wrong, again, as it is possible to be. Tell me about your child as we walk to see them." Lifting two cloaks from a bench and dropping one around the mother's shoulders they left the building out into the cold rain.

15 'Goyim', still in use today, is an insulting word for non-Jew. Go to: https://www. urbandictionary.com/define.php?term=goyim

16 There is discussion about the role and gender of apothecaries. Other titles include 'confectioner' and 'compounder'. The products they made could be both ritual and medicinal and included perfumes, oils and ointments.

The working woman

She was so tired. She knew she should go round the backs of the houses to her tiny home, but she just wanted to get there - wash, eat, sleep. Her daughter would be safe at her grandmother's house tonight.

Her legs ached, her shoulders were sore where one man had grabbed her too hard - a care less, greedy, ugly idiot. She smelled fresh bread. Did she dare? She longed for its crisp crust and soft inside dipped in smooth green oil, or, even, her mother's gently cooked lamb with mint. She stepped into the square, coin ready. Reaching the stall, she lifted a small loaf and gave the scowling trader his money - she recognised him from the last time he paid her. Bread in her bag, head down, she hurried to the alley out of the square. The hate and fear were like a fast-moving thick fog - it caught her with a yell and a rock, sharp, in the middle of her back.

A man, weary from a long day, Yeshua, heard the screams, and ran holding the edge of his gown off of the ground. Screams mixed with laughter and shouts. Coming out from the narrow space between homes he saw them - a crowd of men, pushing, picking up stones and throwing. What at? He got closer, pushed, and pummelled his way through. On the ground, her face cut, was a woman. As well as blood there was bright beautiful colour, red, on her lips. The men were shouting, full of spit and disgust, clenched faces, trying to hurt her and enjoying it. He went straight to her, knelt, put his arm around her, his body a shield. A stone hit him - the person who threw it grimaced when he saw who he had hit. "I'm sorry, so sorry but she's a bad woman."

Holding the woman, he stood and looked at each of them, slowly. "Which of you has paid this woman for what she offers so she can feed her child? Which of you has looked at her and thought how much you want to buy her, but your wife might know? If you can say no to these questions, you can throw a stone otherwise pay her now for her pain and go home - now!" He held out his hand and some men put coins into his hand and walked away. One man, fists bunched, came to him, spit flying off his lips, shoving his face close to the rescuer – "Ha, so you've never wanted her or another woman?" Yeshua spoke, "I never said that - I am a man like you."

Someone came out of a house with a blanket and wrapped it around the hurt woman; someone else came with a jug of wine and some cups. They all sat and drank before walking, together, to the woman's tiny home.

Three ways to annoy the Romans[17]

Give them your coat.

Zak laughed so much that tears slid down his cheeks and into his dark beard. He drank some wine and, laughing still, choked. His friend, Isaac, banged him on his back to help. "Owwwie enough, enough already - stop." He looked at the faces of his friends and neighbours sitting around with jugs of wine almost empty - it had been a very long time since he had seen them smile and laugh so much - their cares dropped for a while. David, a bundle of clothes on the bench next to him, pulled a cloak close around him. The owner of the drinking house came to their tables with two more full jugs. "What's so funny?"

Zak looked at him – "you haven't heard? Sit, come on, sit and I'll tell you." The man wiped his wine and sweat sticky hands down the side of his gown and sat, pouring wine for himself.

"You know David here? He couldn't pay all his tax to that collector with the whip - he just didn't have it. Today he had to go to the court and give even his coat to pay the tax - his coat can you believe! So, I told him, before he went in, what I'd heard that new rabbi saying - you know the one who says the kingdom of heaven is here now, for everyone. He said," Zak snorted, grinned, and shook his head, "if you've got debts and the court demands your coat, which they can, give it to them but also give them your gown and whatever else you're wearing, even your pants! The judges, the tax collector will be sooo embarrassed, humiliated when you stand there with nothing on that they might just let you go - even if they don't you will definitely, definitely have made your point about the shame of what they do. Well, strike me, that's what David did - he'd had enough of being made to feel rubbish. We didn't know he was going to do it and we were waiting outside the court to cheer him up when we heard laughing, shouting and out he came - completely naked, smiling and waving his arms over his head like he'd just won a prize - we roared, he whooped and then he's almost knocked over as his clothes were thrown after him. I rushed up pulling my cloak round him and we carried him here on our shoulders - though how we did that I don't know when we're laughing so much and shouting out what he'd done." The drinking house owner grinned, laughed, and banged the table hard with the palms of his hands and stood up – "this man, David, and his family, can eat and drink here for free as long as they need to and right now it's a drink for everyone." The place erupted with cheers. David, quietly, said, "can I get dressed now?"

Turn your face.

Before it was light, Abihu had gone to check the ties on the gate in the fence that kept the goats in. Today his daughter and his son would have to walk around the fences watching, all day, ready for wolves, eagles and other hungry thieves. Today he had to be elsewhere. The soldiers had stopped him and his friends as they came home from the Temple. "Heh you, in two days be at the warehouses to load our carts, we're off from here, at last. A dinari a day." So, with bread and hard cheese wrapped in a cloth, with a flask of wine and water in his bag Abihu walked as the sun brightened and the trees, rocks and hills took pale green, grey and brown shape. A hawk circled on rising air. He met his friends as they came down paths from their homes to the road to the town. They each had so much to do in their own work that couldn't be left but had to be - there was no saying no to a Roman.

As they walked, they woke up more and talked. Ishmael said that, after Temple a few days before the Romans ordered them to work, he had sat with that new rabbi who was going round with a crowd of friends saying all sorts of different, interesting, and dangerous things. Abihu moved closer to hear. Ishmael said, "Look, the man said that you can't always fight the Romans with spears and knives - there are other ways to do it that might shake their power and our fear." Someone said, "How? What?" Ishmael paused and they all hung back with him. "Mmmm...you know when they hit us on the face? They are only allowed to slap with one hand on one side of our face - the other hand, the left, is unclean. If we turn our faces to offer the other cheek it will make them stop or, at least, hesitate - confused perhaps when they can't strike. They can't break their own rules - at least not in public." Someone said, "who would dare even that?" Abihu tightened his jaw, clenched his teeth - he had been slapped too many times and if there was a way to stop it maybe he would. Ishmael saw his face harden and nodded and they walked on. Abihu felt the fluttering of fear in his belly - could he dare? Outside the warehouses there was a queue of carts with pairs of oxen harnessed into their broad, tapered, and splintery shafts. The thick wooden doors slashed across with metal bars and square nails stood, wide open, the space behind dark, cavernous, forbidden.

A line of men waited, silent. Some carts were thick with straw - Abihu thought, that means heavy lifting of fragile amphora full of oil or posca[18]. He knew there would also be locked crates of swords and arrows, bundles of spears and heaps of digging, building and measuring tools - none of it easy to lift and move especially on a bright hot day with the threat of a slap always hovering. The line began to move. Abihu walked behind Ishmael. There was shouting and thumping as crates were lifted, moved, and placed, and soldiers, impatient to be gone, ordered men to do what they would not do themselves. Abihu and Ishmael came next to carefully leaning lines of clay amphora with dribbles of oil and posca on their dusty outsides. "You, move these to the straw filled carts." They grabbed a handle each, lifted and then gripped the base carrying each amphora horizontally before pushing it into the waiting hands in the carts to be nestled in the still scented dried grasses. It was like lifting rocks. The sixth one they carried was bigger and heavier - it was full of posca and was to be put into the rear of a cart to be easily unloaded and shared out on the road. In front of Abihu and Ishmael, watched by a soldier, a man walked with his arms hugging a bundle of spears. As he went out into the hot sunlight a spear slipped from his encircling arms and went quickly between his legs. He tripped, fell and the spears scattered - some with their dagger points tipped towards Abihu who stopped suddenly, jerking Ishmael's grip. The amphora fell and the handle Abihu held snapped as it hit the ground but the whole giant flask didn't break. A soldier rushed at him shouting, right hand raised. Ishmael watched. Abihu spread his feet apart so as not to fall from the blow but then, looking straight into the soldier's furious, helmeted face, turned his head, the other cheek, and the soldier stopped, grabbed Abihu's head to turn it back but couldn't and stepped away looking for help. Ishmael smiled. Abihu, his heart thumping, bent to pick up the amphora with his friend's aid.

Walking sabotage

The man with the lumpy twisted spine fell, hard, on the gravelly ground. The skin on his knees broke and the rocks in the basket hung on his back tumbled over his shoulders - some smashed onto the backs of his hands spread out to hold his fall. He cried out. The soldier who had tripped him laughed. Other men, still with rock on their backs, rushed, clumsily, to help him, lifting him up. The soldier moved to hit them but stopped as their hands reached for rocks, their eyes like stone. Of course, they knew, if they did throw, they would die, probably hung up at the roadside, but the rage and fury was there, still. Picking up and loading the fallen man's burden they walked on, taking rock to where the road was being mended after heavy rain and cartwheels broke it.

Later, the same men stopped to eat and drink, their empty rock baskets laid aside in a heap. One of them, Saul, said, "It's easier to carry rock than put up with how they treat us. I hate it, I'm useless. If we didn't do the G'd forsaken work, who would they get to do it - themselves? They can eat their own shit and drink their own piss!"[19] A man at the edge of the group, Solomon, said, "maybe it's not G'd forsaken." They looked at him, startled and somebody asked, "what do you mean?" "Well, I heard a man talking who said G'd is always with us in good or bad times, in the Temple or out of it." Some men gasped, looked around, frightened, making sure there was no priest nearby. Solomon continued, "just now we all helped our friend off the ground, whatever the soldier thought or threatened - simple kindness you might say or maybe G'd, love from us." He stopped, smiled as if embarrassed by how he had spoken. He continued though, "we know they have a rule that says we can't stop work until told to - we ignored it, and nothing happened. Supposing we did that again but, this time, turned their rules upside down? Look, this road is broken all the way over the hill and down to the next town - men are carrying rock from the other end, like us. Another Roman rule says we, paid drudges, can only carry our loads for a mile and then have to stop. What if we carried on until we met the men coming the other way? It was an idea from the man I listened to. It would help the others and seriously confuse the guards. What could they do? It also might be very funny to try and cheer us up."

The bored soldiers by the quarry, watching men load and carry grabbed their spears and looked up the road towards the echoing sound of shouts. The line of rock carriers had gone over the hill - too far - and they weren't stopping. A soldier, leather and metal armour flapping and flashing came running, tripping, stumbling. "They won't stop, they keep walking and then tipping their rocks where the other men should - they've even been singing as if they're enjoying it. It's not good."

"What's not good?" said a man putting on a plumed helmet as he stepped, blinking, from a red and gold tent in the shade of a tree that leant out from a crest by the quarry. The line of rock carriers with empty baskets was snaking its way down the road - they were all smiling.

17 Walter Wink is an American theologian, a progressive Christian. He was a member of the Jesus Seminar, an academic group exploring the 'historical Jesus'. In his1992 book 'Beyond Just war and pacifism: Jesus' nonviolent way' he describes how the original resistance to power message in much of the teaching of the man Jesus/Yeshua was revised and negated by a Church embedded in state and imperial power. For example, a teaching most used to deride and ridicule Christian responses to social injustice, violence and war is 'turn the other cheek' here transformed. The other two here are 'carry your

burden an extra mile' and 'if someone takes away your coat give them your shirt as well'.

18 'Posca' could be said to be the Roman military equivalent of 'Red Bull' or runners hydration drinks. Its ingredients were various mixtures of wine vinegar or wine with water and may also have included herbs or spices such as myrrh which has analgesic, pain relieving qualities.

19 I wanted swearing that might match working class fury at mistreatment. This is an adaptation of a translation of an exchange in the book of Kings - 18:27. In other translations it's much more politely put!

A surprising day

A child is sitting quietly on the ground outside of his house. The
building is small, square shaped and muddy coloured. The ground is
dusty, and the day is beginning to be hot. The child, Jacob, has eaten
some bread and dates and drunk some sheep's milk. He is waiting for
his mum and dad to finish jobs they are doing. The day is a special day,
its Seder, the Passover, and lots of his family are coming later to share
in the Seder meal. Jacob is going to help with the meal, and, for the
first time, he has a prayer to say. He's excited and nervous. As he sits
dreaming about the day he hears the sound of people walking up the
path to his house. The path is stony, so footsteps are crunchy and noisy.
A big, dark bird, disturbed by the walkers, cries out, flies off flapping
hard against leaves and branches of the tree it had sheltered in. Jacob
watches and sees two men. Oddly, they don't come straight to the
house but walk towards the little open fronted stable where the family's
two donkeys shelter. One of the men starts to loosen the rope that ties
the youngest, untrained, donkey to a black metal ring in the wall.

Jacob jumps up, runs to the doorway of the house. He shouts, "mum,
dad, two men are stealing our donkey, two men are stealing our
donkey!" His mum rushes out with flour on her hands and arms and
wielding a meat knife. His dad comes out and picks up an axe leaning
on some logs by the door. They run, shouting, to the stable. The two
men, shocked and scared, step back from the donkey and hold up their
hands - their palms - towards the angry family. One of the men, still
looking very scared, words tumbling out, says, "I'm sorry, I'm sorry, our
rebe, our teacher, the man Yeshua, he said to tell you that he needed a
donkey today, he is going into the town. He thought you wouldn't mind.
We didn't think – we're used to automatically sharing. We were going to
come to your door before we left."

Immediately the mum and dad stop – she holds the knife to her side
and he, holding the handle, lets the axe rest the top of its sharp head on

the ground. She says, "oh sorry, I wish you'd come to the house first – it would have saved our anger and you being so scared." She is still a bit cross. She takes a big breath, in and out, slowly, and says, "I've heard your rabbi talking and the things I heard him say," she hesitated and looked at her husband, "well, they touched my heart. He is right, I don't mind because, trusting him, I trust you to bring our donkey back." She again looked toward her husband for his acceptance, and he nodded. She walked toward the donkeys and began to untie the older, trained donkey. One of the men said, "Thank you, thank you but Yeshua was very clear, he said to bring him your youngest, untrained donkey, the foal, the child of your eldest." The mum is surprised but unties the youngest and gives the rope to one of the men. The men turn to walk away.

Jacob cannot contain himself any longer. He bursts out with excitement about what is happening, forgetting anything else he might have to do. He grabs his mum's hand, "mum, please, please, can I go. I could help with the donkey. Please, oh please." His mum looks at his dad – doubtful, about to say no when one of the men, smiling, says, "let him come, he can hold the donkey's rope and lead it through any crowds. We will both keep our eyes on him." It would be a big thing to say yes, there will be soldiers out – this is a big day for Jewish people and the soldiers will be edgy and ready to attack if they see or imagine somebody is starting trouble, challenging the power of the army and the king. It is a time to be careful, yes, but it is also a time to trust friends and neighbours and to spot the good in people. It is quiet whilst Jacob's mum and dad think; they talk quietly, and he knows to be silent – that's hard. After a few minutes his dad holds Jacob's hand, quite tightly, and says, "you can go but you must stay with our donkey and keep it safe, you must listen to what our two new friends here say or to what the rabbi tells you. No going off by yourself and be back here in time for our Seder – whatever happens you have things to do here with your family."

Jacob, for a moment, is without words. Then jumping up and down, he hugs his dad, his mum, grins at the two smiling men and even hugs the donkey. Running indoors to get a water bottle, some more bread and some dates he remembers to ask the men if they are thirsty – they are. He brings them a bowl of water to share that has been kept covered, cool in a shady place by their well. Jacob, ready now, takes the rope on the youngest donkey from the man's hand and walks between the two men, turns just once to smile at his parents and give a small wave.

They walk for about half an hour from his home until they come to a grove of trees. A small crowd of women and men sit resting in the shade. One of them, a man with long dark hair, stands and comes towards Jacob. Stopping, he looks at him for a moment, smiles and says, "thank you for bringing your donkey. It's as big a day for you both as it is likely to be for me. Come and sit for a while." Jacob ties his donkey to a bush and sits. Everybody smiles at him. He is the only child there.

Soon it's time to go. They leave the safe shelter of the trees. A blanket is laid across the donkey's back - Jacob holds the rope whilst Yeshua, the man with long dark hair, sits on the donkey and begins to ride. Jacob feels excited. First of all, the road just has people walking with their friends or family but soon, as people, up and down the road, hear that Yeshua is there they start to crowd together. They watch or walk alongside Yeshua and his friends (and Jacob and the donkey) and they become more and more excited – smiling, waving, and talking. A man in the crowd, another rabbi, calls out loudly like he might burst; "everybody, listen, shout, all of you from Yerushalayim! Look, look who is coming. This man can help us, he's like a king but so different - good and humble – see, look, look he rides a donkey, oh not even a donkey, the foal of a donkey, not like those on the other side of the city today." People join in, shouting and singing, 'Hosanna, hosanna.'[20] Many people think, hope, that this man is a leader who can help them beat the soldiers, the Romans. Jacob holds the donkey's rope a little more tightly and whispers softly to him to keep him calm in the noise. Jacob hears the two men talking – "this is amazing. I have never seen people turn out like this. It's like they are saying, here we are, we don't care, and we're going to say what we want." The other man said, "This is more than a walk. This is a big challenge to the soldiers, the Romans, to the powers. I'm afraid."

Jacob notices that Yeshua isn't excited. He doesn't behave like a strong, proud or bossy leader. He's not calling out or waving. He is still as he rides. People put branches of palm trees on the road in front of the donkey and its rider. Other people lay their cloaks down on the road. Jacob thinks, It's like they think this man is a king. Some people rush forward; Jacob thinks they are from the Temple, maybe those people called Levites. They usually help the Romans. Some of them call out, "tell these people to be quiet, ssshh, sssshh. What they are saying is wrong - dangerous." But, Yeshua, speaking for the first time, says, loudly, "if these people become quiet then the very stones in the ground will cry out for them and their pain and suffering."

Jacob keeps walking. Just before they get to the city Yeshua speaks quietly to him, "please, stop for a moment." The donkey halts and Yeshua sits still. Jacob, looking up, sees that he is crying. He hears him say, softly, as if talking to the city and nobody nearby, "oh, if only you had listened and heard what could make peace happen, but you didn't, you wouldn't and now it's hidden again and you'll be knocked down, destroyed." Yeshua asks Jacob to walk a little further with the donkey through a curved gate into the city. Jacob thinks the man looks sad – this is a puzzle for him. Why is he sad? People still call out "hosanna, hosanna." Once inside the high city wall Yeshua, a bit sore, climbs off the little donkey, turns to Jacob, and says, "thank you for your donkey and your help – please, remember today." He then asks one of the men to walk with the child back to his home. Yeshua walks on with his friends in the middle of the crowd.

Jacob's mum and dad have the house ready for Seder - the table is laid out and the food is all ready, waiting for their family. They hug and hold Jacob when they see him and thank the man. Jacob ties up the donkey, strokes him and gives him water and food. He tells his mum and dad all about his day – two times! They love to hear about what he has heard and seen. They hold him, tight, again, as if to keep him safe. In the evening, he says his Seder prayer really well and, somehow, it comes out stronger because of his day.

20 *Hosanna, in most Christian practice, has come to mean and to be used as a word of praise for the 'king'. Earlier, Hebrew, usage has meanings of save, help or rescue – it's an appeal in times of hardship or oppression, an expression of hope for the coming of someone who might just be able to help. See 'The old soldier' story' for more context.*

Tables in a temple

Once there was a woman called Bilha.

Bilha speaks:

"Oh, good it's a sunny morning. My oh my, I've got achy arms and back. All that cooking and serving and standing for everybody who came to the party was great to do, but now my poor old body hurts. Thank G'd I have a chance for some quiet, prayer and a little rest today when I go to the Temple. It'll make a change from our little synagogue – I won't have to chat with anybody or hear anybody's worries or problems. Just me. I'll take some bread, dates and some of that special cheese. Off I go. Hopefully I'll get that quiet place that's tucked away to the side of the Temple next to a big cupboard that doesn't get used much. Just enough room to put my little mat on the floor to stop my knees and bottom getting sore when I pray or sit.

Here we are, that didn't take long. Wow, I've never seen it so busy. Still my little place looks empty. I'll just squeeze my way through the crowds and get comfy and quiet. Lovely. My special blue scarf over my head feels cosy – somehow it helps me feel extra quiet."

She sits.

In the Temple there's a worker called Dawid.

Dawid speaks:

"I'm Dawid. I work in the Temple. I clean, carry water, and do any jobs that need doing that priests or rabbis won't do. Today I'm very busy – it's hot, noisy and people are thirsty. I see that quiet, gentle woman with the blue scarf is in to pray. She is over near the store cupboard. She always looks so peaceful. I wish I had a quiet time like she does. Wait! What's happening? A man with a cage of pigeons and other stuff to sell is shouting at her to move and he's shoving his table at her where she's kneeling. Now she's fallen over, and her food has spilt out of her bag. She's lying on the floor; she looks shocked and hurting. The man is not helping her at all and is shouting calling her 'a stupid woman.' I'm going over – this is very, very bad. Hang on, what's happening now?"

Dawid turns towards the entrance of the Temple; the great doors are wide open. There's a crowd shouting and pushing. Then he sees a tall man with long dark hair. The crowd moves away from him. Dawid thinks he saw him the other day riding on a donkey into the city and people threw palm leaves and their cloaks onto the ground for him. The man goes to the tables where people are selling pigeons, food and changing people's valuable coins into smaller amounts of money – they make them pay to do this.[21] He grabs the front edge of each table and tips them over, one by one with a crash – the pigeons fly out of broken cages and escape the Temple, money spills to the floor, food is scattered. Dawid hears the man shout, "This is G'd's house. You turn it into a den for cruel, unjust people who think they can say a prayer, give money or an animal, and get away with the harm they do. Get out. Get out!" He is in such a fury that no one stops him. Dawid sees a priest hold up his hand to stop a Roman soldier arresting the man. The priest has a thin, spiteful smile on his face. The man, his name, Dawid remembers, is Yeshua, comes towards Dawid – he's seen the pigeon seller and the woman. Dawid goes to Yeshua and walks alongside him – somehow it makes him feel unafraid. When they get to where the woman is still on the floor the pigeon seller runs away. Yeshua helps Bilha up, picks up and gives her the blue scarf from the floor. Dawid puts her food back in her bag. Yeshua, and Dawid, sit on the floor with Bilha – everything goes quiet around them. Bilha softly says a thankyou prayer – "I offer thanks to you, our G'd, for you have mercifully restored my soul within me; Your faithfulness is great" - Modeh ani lefaneḥa meleḥ ḥai vekayam, she'he'ḥezarta bee nishmatee b'ḥemla, raba emunatecha[22]. The two men repeat the words as she says them.

21 Traditionally Yeshua is depicted as turning the tables of the 'money changers' (is this an anti-Semitic trope?) – it is also commonly used as an attack on capitalist-oriented church hierarchies. In fact, the synagogue practice of changing coin from Roman to acceptable Jewish currency and selling animals

for sacrifice was legitimate whilst, of course benefitting temple finance. Marcus Borg, another member of the Jesus Seminar (see Epilogue) suggests a more complex attack on hypocrisy and pretence.

22 Prayer sourced from PJLibrary.org, an American Jewish resources provider.

A lost friend

Once there was man called Judas.

Judas speaks:

"I don't know if anybody will find this, but I am going to write it anyway. Terrible things have happened, and I know people will say horrible things about me – some maybe true in a way but I want to leave my story of what went on, who did what and what I did. I am going to try to write it as I saw things, not changing what happened to make myself look better. So here it is – well at least some of it. It is hard, at the end, to describe my desperation, regret and fear."

Watching a miracle.

"It's a sunny day. I'm sitting on a hillside to the edge of a great crowd – children, women and men, everybody. Noise, excitement. I can see children getting lost and being found. There are some people begging at the edge of the crowd asking for a coin, a drink, a piece of bread. There's a man sneaking about trying to steal from people who look richer – maybe from people working for the Temple or the hated Romans. My master, the rebe called Yeshua, has been talking but is resting now. Apart from what he has done here he has had a terrible day with the news about his cousin.

He's looking around and he's turning to one of the people closest to him - ohh its bossy, loud speaking Yohanan, always thinking he's the better person, special friend to Yeshua. It's worse – he's coming over to me! Right now, I don't want to speak to anyone. I'm trying to think. I don't know what to do. Yeshua has been talking about heaven being here on earth, how poor people are strong and rich people weak, can be nearer to and further from G'd, but I need him to say more, to make more happen. Look, here are, maybe, 5,000 people listening to him, come to hear him. An army. If he would only say, 'the time has come, pick up a sword, an axe, a knife, a rock and attack and destroy the Roman army.'

I love listening to him speak. Somehow what he says warms me up, makes me feel both safe and powerful and even dangerous in a funny way. I want to run around shouting, listen, listen, listen to what Yeshua is saying – open your ears, your brain, and your dreams. Everything can be better. There is no more need for fear, hatred and even hunger. But it's not enough for me – I feel pulled in two. Oh, and now here is Yohanan standing over me – why does he loom so? 'Judas, Yeshua says we have to feed everybody; they're hungry and you have the money.' I look around, it's hot, there are so many people – how can we feed them all? As I'm looking and wondering how on earth I can do this I notice something happening. The crowd has turned to Yeshua. He's speaking and holding up a small basket and there's a child standing close to him. What is he doing? Who is the child? Yeshua is taking some food from the basket and giving pieces of it to the child and to people near him. Suddenly, it's like a ripple, a wave through the crowd. People who have some food are turning to their neighbours and offering them some. Oh my – it's happened again. Without doing very much Yeshua has got people to break the rules – the food rules say don't share food unless you know where it comes from. He's ignoring it to make sure no one goes hungry. Some men, Temple priests or people working with the Romans, at the edge of the crowd are talking and looking angry – huh, what do they care, they make sure they never go hungry! I look up at Yohanan who seems to be confused – he no longer has to feed people so can't show off and he is trying to understand what just happened. I lie back under the shady tree in the cool air and smile, forgetting how muddled and cross I was for a moment."

Doubt and temptation

"I remember, now, sitting under another tree – this one old and twisted, its few pointed leaves soft green and feathery grey. Another bright day. It was good to sit. We had been walking from one town to another village to another town – talking, helping, listening and, sometimes, arguing about what Yeshua said and did and, once, about whom he liked the most or thought the best. Still, he was telling people to love one another and still he wouldn't call out for people to fight the Romans and the people who worked for them. It made me so angry. The city I came from, Keriah, is famous for soldiers as well as for people studying G'ds law. Both matter. But, every day, by the roadside, there were people, fighters, hung on crosses, some bitten by dogs, hung there by the Romans to scare us. Why doesn't he shout out, Tear down the crosses, rescue the people, push the Romans into the sea. What could I do? How could I get him to change? Could I make him be different – maybe scare him, just a bit, so that he'd think differently like my friends back home hiding in the hills angry, ready to fight? Oh, I didn't want to, I wanted what Yeshua said to be true but everything that is happening hurts people so much that it can't work. Was he right? Was I right? These thoughts were like a storm in the desert when wind blows sand into such high clouds and swirls that you can't see and it stings, bites and hurts.

I got up and walked back into the town by myself. Yeshua was resting in the house of some friends and everybody else was having time alone and quiet. I wanted some food. Some soldiers, not Temple guards, were standing on the street. I stopped close to listen to what they were saying – they looked worked up. One of them said, 'that man, the dangerous one they call Yeshua, I've heard the Chief Priest wants to catch but can't ever find him. He's always moving and people give him shelter in their homes. We have to find him and give money to anybody who helps us.' I went across the yellowy dusty street to a tiny shop and bought some fresh, soft bread and dried fish. When the soldiers walked away I carefully followed. They went into a building that was a place for soldiers to eat and sleep and to keep prisoners. I heard someone scream and cry. I needed to work out what to do. If Yeshua got into trouble it might make him think, 'that's enough, time to fight.' I'll do it, I'll go in, and I'll tell them where they can find him.

The day had been hot, the street smelt of rotting, mouldy fruit and vegetables and sheep dung. I went into the building. It was cool and a bit dark inside. The soldier by the door gripped his sword and shouted, 'what do you want here Jew?' I thought, 'Uh oh I'm in real trouble' but I kept going. 'I can tell you where you could find the man Yeshua – the one the priests want'. The soldier grabbed my arm hard, just below the shoulder – 'stay here, don't leave!' He rushed off. I heard his voice and a shouted order, 'Bring him here.' He came back, grabbed me again, pulled me, hurting, to a room a bit further into the building. There was a table made of big rough pieces of wood – it still looked like a tree trunk. On the table was a jug of water and a cup – drops of water were like tears down the front of the jug. It looked so cool – that fish had been lovely but salty. The big soldier behind the table didn't offer me any to drink. He stared at me like I was something dirty and stinking that had come into his room. He spoke in a voice that felt like a punch. 'What's your name?' I told him. 'How do you know the man, Yeshua?' I told him. 'Who else is with him?' I told him feeling more and more that this, now, was wrong but too late. 'Will you give Yeshua to us?'

'Yes'. I didn't think they would do anything really bad to him even though the roadsides were full of crosses – too many people liked him. They wouldn't dare. 'Stand up.' The other soldier came in and pulled me by my bruised arm out of the room to the back of the building to a door into an alley. Now I was really, really scared – were they just going to kill me here? They could – they had done it so many times in the back alleys, in the dark – bodies found like broken birds, crows on a wall, a warning to everybody else. 'Where are you taking me?'

'To the priests, those Jews who work for us to keep you lot in line – the ones who pay Herod to pay the Emperor with your money to pay and feed us.' I walked, staggered, up the alley – I'd never been there before; on the right-hand side there were small slit alleys leading off, joining with the main street. Soldiers stood at the top of each of these, stopping anybody they didn't know from getting through. Up a slope and then there was a door – locked. The first soldier had a key. Behind the door was a steep staircase – somehow we had come into the Great Temple. At the top of the steps there is a long empty corridor – at the end of this I was slammed down onto a stone bench; the big soldier walked further in, the other stood by me scratching under the leather armour on his chest – probably lice.

Hope and fear

I remember sitting, waiting, feeling sick, my toes tense, pushing down and my heels high off the floor. After what seemed a long time of empty quiet the big soldier came out and nodded at the other who grabbed me by my sore arm and pulled, dragged me up and pushed me into the room opposite the bench. The light was bright after the corridor. The room smelt of burning perfumed oil – peppery, sweet, hard to breathe. The two soldiers stood at the back leaving me in front of a heavy, red wood table with a smooth, wide top and thick carved legs – again there was water in a jug and a cool clay mug. The man, a priest, behind the table looked at me with eyes like nails – hard and small. He spoke with a voice like a hammer – 'Who are you? How do you think you can help us?' I said my name softly like I didn't want him to hear or remember it; I was bending over, sagging like a dog waiting to be hit. 'I can tell you where to find Yeshua.' The priest smiled – eyes nails, voice hammer, smile a knife – 'I suppose you want money.' 'Not really but I'll take it if you give it.'

I was on the cusp, the edge, of changing my mind – this felt more dangerous than I thought it would – was I a prisoner? Was I going to die, here? If I don't tell them I will certainly die – if I tell them, what then? Maybe it'll work – if Yeshua feels as scared as I do, he'll be angry and fight – maybe. I hear the quieter voice in me saying, you know he won't, you know him – I ignore it. I continued, 'We are meeting soon, somewhere, I don't know where – when I know I'll tell you. I'll find a soldier or a guard to come to you.' The priest said, 'yes, you will because, if you don't, we'll find you, your friends, your family in Kerioth and give them to the Romans.' He opens a box on the table and takes out a small, heavy leather bag and throws it at me. It hits me on the cheek, I bleed. Bending down I pick it up and leave, walking past the soldiers to go to meet my friends, and Yeshua, and not tell them what I've done. Would they guess?

The garden

"This is such a beautiful garden – why have I not spent time here before? Now, when I know that the end and the beginning is almost here, I stand and wait in the shade and perfume of the trees, herbs and flowers. I wish I could just stay here – still, talking to people, helping, telling stories. I don't want the end that I know is coming – I see it almost every day at the roadside, in people's stories. My friends, well the men anyway, really don't believe what I've told them again and again and again is coming and what they will have to do and bear. Miryam, the other women, they know and their sadness is hardest to know; I wish I could stay just with them, in their soft, gentle, strong, protective company. Sometimes, I too, want to be held."

He turns, shakes his head to loosen the hair from his neck. He realises the evening is dark – he's been standing there for a long time. As he turns, he whispers to himself, "please, let me go." He means to walk back to the town to sleep but, in the gloom, he trips and almost falls – it's the sleeping body of one of his friends. His stomach lurches and his heart suddenly tenses and hurts – couldn't they stay awake tonight of all nights when he needs them? In the still air of the garden his voice is suddenly sharp, broken and hollow – "wake, wake up, I told you that you'd desert me and here you are asleep rather than being with me."

They stand, ashamed, their clothes glow in the dark air – they are blocks of light colour next to the black and green slabs of the shadows. Then noise and yellow light – fear loosens their stomachs. Can they run, hide. Its guards shouting – "where is he? Show us, tell us which one." Before they scatter, they reel as if hit – they see their friend Judas, sad-faced, pushed from the guards, stumbling. He goes to Yeshua who smiles softly straight at him. Judas, quickly, hugs and kisses him. He's then grabbed, thrown aside as the guard's grip Yeshua and tie his hands – hitting him hard so that he staggers. A friend thrusts a knife at a guard cutting him – Yeshua shouts, "no, do not do that – put the knife down."

The men run, fearing capture and death. Yeshua resists the pulling of the guards and looks up catching the eyes of the women who have stayed – he shakes his head and they quietly go, weeping but escaping terrible violence.

Yeshua is dragged, pushed and hit by the Temple guards who are laughing, shouting and thinking of how they will spend the money the priests will give them. It's a job well done – what an idiot this man is. Judas, alone in the dark, knows desperately that he's failed.

A kind hand

Beronike had been well for a while now. The room where they all slept no longer had the metal smell of blood in it. She and her husband could hold and touch each other again – the memory made her warm. She could hug her children without flinching with pain or seeing their embarrassment or sadness.

Today she was daydreaming a little, standing making bread – she still got excited and thrilled when the bread rose and then baked so beautifully. It was like she was helping food grow that, in turn, made her children grow. She put the bread into the oven, cleaned the old table that had been her mother's and washed dough and flour off her hands. She held the edge of the table and stretched her back and shoulders – that always felt good after the hard work of mixing, breaking and kneading.

She was thinking about how people can be broken and kneaded and become whole when there was a shout, almost a scream from outside. Running to the door and into the street she met her friend who was crying. "It's him, it's Yeshua, they're going to kill him." Beronike's breath disappeared from her body and her heart hurt like it might stop. "How could they? What has he done? He was so kind to me." She rushed indoors yelling to her husband the news and telling him to watch the bread. She was going, going to see what she could do – at least to stand there as he passed to the hill of skulls. She grabbed a shawl and a scarf, white, for her head and ran, ran to her friend and into the town.

Everywhere there were soldiers – Romans with swords, spears, shields. Temple guards, some smiling, with sticks, knives, and cudgels – all looking hard and ugly. Holding her friend's hand, she pushed and shouted and begged her way through crowds – many people, like her, frightened, tear stained, angry and disbelieving. What would they do without him? He's like the goodness in me – please, please don't hurt him. But, she knew, if they'd decided to kill him, that kindness, mercy would not be in their hearts. She got separated from her friend. She bumped into a man – rich, with a beautiful cloak. She's seen him in the Temple with the priests. He was crying, shaking his head, looking around for help or a friend. Not thinking if it was alright to do, she grasped his hand and smiled at him – more tears rose in his eyes, and he gripped her hand in return.

She burst out of the side street onto the main road leading to the hill. She'd been running so fast that she now found she was through the crowd, and looking down the road. She heard the sound of a whip cracking, some laughter, and some booing.

Now, on the outside of the bumping, ogling, pushing, hard edged crowd she was still. She paused, full of waiting, hearing everything, but not touched; just breathing for a few moments – it was like when she gave birth, towards the end, in the storms of pain, a peculiar calm as of smooth unbroken water. A rock held in deep wet sand, sea coming and going over it – the last rock above the tide. She shook her head, looked down the road and saw him coming, bent at the knees dragging the single beam of the cross. Somebody, quickly, pushed a dripping wet cloth across his broken lips before a soldier could stop her. A young man, weeping, tried to get past guards to lift the tree from the man but was knocked to the ground. Somebody else laughed, pointing, shouting – "some Messiah you are, useless" – disappointment and loss calling out. The moving crowd around Yeshua was full of women, some with their children, heads covered, holding hands – they kept step with the man who was going to die, halting when he stumbled, holding their breath, hands to mouths and on each other, tears run dry, stronger than they ever knew they could be.

As he came near to her, she saw that he was blinking, trying to see, dirt and sweat and dust and tears making him blind and more likely to fall and cut and graze and bruise. She knew with a heart hard with pain that she could do little. He came to where she was, saw her, looked at her and, even there, paused and smiled. She pulled her white scarf from her head, not fearing spear, cudgel, knife, or whip and knelt by him, held his shoulder, gripping with love, and wiped his eyes, his forehead, his cheeks, his mouth and chin and, as a lover might, held and kissed his face and watched him pass.

The old soldier

Lucius sits outside his square, bright white-walled farm on a Tuscan hillside. Tall trees like enormous green feathers line the road away from his home toward the curving, sun shimmered horizon. Warmth draws scent from rosemary spikes into the air. He loves that he has been able to come back to the rich, crumbly red earth and sit in the garden. He's been in dry, burning hot kingdoms across the middle sea and before that in cold, sodden, mud mired forests in the north - far away and stranger still.

What he'd done had bought this place, away from war. The cost, apart from dinari, had been burying, locking up tender, gentle parts of himself - just a soldier, a fighter. Hard, competent, coping. Each time he came home his son, Marcus, thrilled to hear his dad's adventures - never knew anything was different - played with his wooden horse and soldiers.

Now here he is. His wife, Marcella, became ill and died swiftly, soon after he finally came home. Instead of those years he had imagined, he's on his own. By the time he'd retired his son was already in the great city, a long way away, learning to be a centurion like his dad, his life mapped out in straight roads. For Lucius it's all turned around - it's him waiting for the words on a tablet[23] that always take so long to come in their special wrapping to keep them safe. He often sits and wonders what his son is doing - maybe he's already gone far away to rule, fight and punish.

Despite his sadness, his life has goodness and he's not bitter or without purpose. He spends his days on and around his farm, telling people what to do and hoping they don't notice, too much, that he pretends to know all about the work when sometimes he doesn't. He smiles when he thinks about the man who brings the bread - he is in love with one of his women servants and visits a lot bringing special cakes for her and Lucius. Lucius knows he must free her so that they can marry or at least share a house.

Sometimes he walks checking walls and fences, looking at everything growing - grapes, olives, wheat, barley, beans, broccoli, onions. Along a wall pears are spread out on carefully tended branches. In a small yard chickens squabble around the base of the dovecote full of fluttering. Some days friends visit, and they drink soft, red, watered wine and eat honey cakes.

Late one day at dusk, he sits, softened by wine, slipping into an easy doze. He has been thinking about his own twilight, ending. Dreaming on the edges of sleep, memories blend in and he wakes suddenly, shaken, sweating. Momentarily fearing he's ill, blocking memory, he calls out but, as his oldest servant, Gallio, rushes to him, waves him away, snapping – "it's only a dream." Back in the kitchen Gallio says to his wife, "another dream."

He sits as heart beating panic subsides and knows, without really thinking, that now he's not busy all the time there is space, somehow, inside him for unbidden remembering and there is something knotted, tight, lurking and untold reawakening. As a soldier armoured outside and in, there was, he was thankful, no time for this to happen. But now, he knows, whatever the battles, policing, torture, destruction, executions and crucifixions, all of the soldiers he'd commanded and people he'd disappeared or made slaves, amidst all of that one remembrance has lodged, hammered home. He reaches for the still cool jug of wine and pours cups until it's empty. Not now, he thinks, not now - I will not allow this, and, anyway, who could I tell. Standing, knocking over his stool, he goes, hoping he can sleep. The recollection, however, doesn't go away.

One morning sitting outside near thick bushes of thyme and bay with a cup of warm spiced wine, a wooden plate of soft new bread, some dates and a clay bowl of thin honey, he hears the crunching footsteps of the man bringing bread and cakes but this time he comes to the garden. Bowing his head, suddenly fearful of the often stern old soldier, the baker says, "a rider came through the village, sir, asking for you. I said I could bring you his package - I hope I wasn't wrong." Lucius could easily have been angry, but he just wants the red dust covered, soft leather bundle in his hands and to be by himself, so shaking his head says, "thank you." He unties and peels open what he hopes is word from Marcus. He hates it, but he's missed him. He holds the tablets[23] like treasure.

Later he strides hard and fast on the path bounding his fields. He slashes at plants, anything, with a pole from the vines - seed heads, flowers, stalks scatter. Workers in the fields know to keep away - the stick might just as well flail them. "By Mars," he mutters to himself, "how is this? Now, now I hear he is in Judaea just as I am infested by the memory, cockroaches crawling in my mind."

He arrives, late, back at the house and leans the pole against a wall. On the table outside near the thyme and bay there is a bowl of water scented with floating lemon and lavender - Gallio had watched for him. He washes his face and dries with a waiting white cloth. Gallio comes out with pigeons cooked in onions, garlic and olives, some bread and a jug of their new wine. Neither speaks but Gallio stands as Lucius eats. If Marcella were here she would gentle his troubles out of him but she isn't. He looks at Gallio who smiles kindly – "you have to tell Marcus, whatever it is." Lucius shakes his head and smiles back – "how do you always know?" Gallio clears the plates. In the morning Lucius sends for a scribe and pays, and threatens him, with more than he ever imagined, to write what Lucius says and keep it secret.

This is what was written:

"When I finished reading what you sent me the last time it took me to, what feels like, the end of a knotted ball of thread inside me. Your words somehow tugged on the end of this thread and helped an unravelling that had already begun. So, what is it? There is something that happened when I was in Judaea that I've not heard anyone else talk about except maybe bits of chat I overheard from other older soldiers but never joined in. I'm old and now, especially as your mother is dead, I don't have anyone else, apart from you, to tell. Gallio, of course, knows something is wrong but I can't begin to tell him - he has been my servant for too long and I can't let down my guard as much as I would need to. The scribe writing this has been well paid and also knows what would happen to him and his family if he ever told. I know some of this is close to treason.

When I used to come home I only wanted to tell you about forts, people painted blue, dark forests, warriors who were never afraid, hot sandy places, fighting. These were the stories I wanted you to hear; it's like they were about the person you and your mother expected me to be, I was sure I was. But I am haunted by one story and I want the haunting to stop. Maybe, if I bring it into the air, it'll be at rest.

I was in Judaea. It was a hard, bright shining day. The breast plate on my uniform was burning hot and the sun's glinting dazzled the eyes of people watching. My cohort circled the king and my generals – a closed fist of power. We had marched for days to be ready for the great procession into the city. We were the 1000 soldiers ready to destroy the shabby, Jew cowards hiding in the hills who dared to fight with knives, axes, rocks and spears. We would be like a knife through cooked meat, the hammer on a nail through a hand. We had been told that today on the other side of the city a crowd was going to be walking with a new leader - what do they think they can do?

In front of us the priests, some carrying the High Priest, others roaring hoarse calls to worship on the ram's horn shofars. Lines of soldiers with great circular polished cornu wrapped around them and straight tuba joined with them in a sharp, blasted out metal cacophony that hurt the ears and made you think a battle was coming.[24] It was a good day for putting your foot on a shepherd's face and stealing his children. I wanted them to try something stupid so we could show them who we are - again.

Days later my commander came to me in my bare room in the stone barracks behind the warehouses. He said, 'the High priest has a prisoner who has to be broken, and I thought of you and what you are good at - it's a man who has been causing trouble.' I had humiliated, wounded, killed, and driven mad so many people that I couldn't remember. I was casually used to hurting and terrifying people - children, women, men - it was easy, and I always tried to do what I was ordered.

The Temple was full of the stench of the slaughtered, eviscerated animals and birds burning, sacrificed on multiple altars. In a back room away from people's hearing I took turns in beating and half drowning the man. I'd heard other soldiers say people called him a rescuer, a rabbi blessed by their god, a teller of stories - well, whatever, now he was just half naked, wet, cut and bleeding and there was only going to be one ending.

I left the room to eat and then stationed myself where the priests waited - others could continue the breaking; we could destroy cities; one man was nothing.

As I am now compelled to observe my life in reverse, I see that this moment is when I could have paused and considered why is this man so dangerous that we break him for the priests? Why not do what we have always done - condemn and kill? I was usually good at strategy but in the moment of elated power I forgot to wonder what my commanders and the collaborator priests and rulers were thinking. Why not ignore him? Were they scared? Could I have changed what happened? Made it quicker, forgettable. Very soon though, it was too late.

I felt unusually uncertain. The dark cedarwood doors opened. The man was thrown into the room and then dragged by his bent elbows, knees scraping, in front of the High Priest who was stiff and outwardly clean, in gold, white and blue, contrasting the filthy, dark blood stained almost corpse in front of him. The priest's eyes were like the stone of the Temple. But something was wrong - I could always tell, even in the middle of pain and blood-soaked wreckage when a battle was being lost, and fleeing or desperate acts of terror were needed. The man just didn't seem scared - even if he was. On his knees he paused before he stood licking drops of water still trickling down his face, thirsty. I stepped forward, looked at the priest, and then hit the man with the side of my sword on his shoulders, slapping. Somebody in the room gasped. The man bent his head to the floor, almost praying, and then stood, slowly, hurting hands on his knees pushing himself up. He looked at every face in front of him and even mine just to the left side - he seemed to look longer at me. Momentarily I felt sorrow somehow pushed into me, as if there was a fracture in the metal and leather in which I was immured. I hit him again - this time just because I wanted to. He didn't fall but rocked.

'Well,' said the priest, 'you are definitely a tricky one. Nothing we have said or done has caught you. Everyone I sent to catch you out came back confused, embarrassed or humbled. Well, not me - you will answer what I ask.' The man replied, 'I will'. I took a step forward, but the priest held his palm towards me, and I moved back. To another question[25] the man answered, 'I am.' I knew, and I am certain the priest did, that the words the man used could be both a 'yes' and a question – 'I will or 'I will?', 'I am' or 'I am?' He was clever and he was doing what he had done all along - not giving in or falling into a trap, even now. The priest, like any torturer, decided to believe what he wanted or needed to and said, 'he has condemned himself'. Pretending that he couldn't possibly be involved in something as unclean as a man's death he handed the prisoner to the city rulers, who in turn, caring less, asked a crowd to decide what happened to him. I knew that most of the crowd outside were Temple workers, angry merchants or otherwise in the pay of the priests or other powers – not people who'd walked with him – so the decision was sure.

I gripped his upper arm hard to leave more blood pinches and as if he might run. Then, he stopped; I can still feel it, his left foot forward flat and firm, his right foot back, a little, and bracing - a fighting stance.

For a moment he was immoveable. Looking at me, ignoring the room, he said, 'Is this all you do?' It wasn't contempt, bravado or ridicule. In that room of hatred, condemnation, and violence he looked at me bewildered and disappointed, strangely kind. I felt as if what I did, and had always done, was dust, dry, settled in the bottom of a dark, empty bowl. The bruise of those few words, it turns out, never healed. I remember he sighed, looked down and walked forwards, somehow sunken and sad. I wished I had more time to hurt him. I still held his arm and stepped with him through a door onto a balcony in sharp sunlight as the crowd roared, baying for death.

He died, almost alone, hammered to wood, his only company some useless women who wouldn't leave - oh and one soldier who soaked a cloth in herb enthused posca - I whipped and punched him for his disobedience.[26] This is all I have to say. I will give this to you when you come home or leave it safe with a notary if I die before you return."

Marcus was exhausted and the scar of the sword stab in his left abdomen just under the ribs was stretched and twisted as he rode his horse - it pulsed and ached; he feared it would tear open, again. He hadn't expected to come home so soon, but with the punishment, wrecking and destruction of the city he used to patrol completed, many of them had been released - for a time. Now, on the dusty, red road curving through the high, plumed trees to his home he wondered what it would be like not to go back - war felt far away. On the hillside ahead he could see the farm and thought there were two people standing, waiting in the sun.

Gallio, holding the reins once the horse is still, hands Marcus a cup of cool, deep - red wine. He drinks in the welcome and steps down into the arms of his father - it's a brief flooding proximity and with it he is home.

23 *Tablets were made of thin sheets of wood or wax. For some purposes they could be said to be like a 'postcard'. A trove of these was found, and continues to be uncovered, at Vindolanda in northern England and many are like 'dear mum, thanks for the socks' or 'thanks for the party, when are you visiting?' See: https://en.wikipedia.org/wiki/Vindolanda_tablets*

24 *Cornu and tuba were instruments used for communication in battle. To see what they looked like go to: https://www.flickr.com/photos/pic_joy/5099888124*

25 *A question asked by a priest is alleged to have been something like, 'are you the son of g-d' – meaning do you claim divinity for yourself? In recent history that might equally have been are you a terrorist, are you a communist or antisemitic?*

26 *The traditional narrative is of a Roman soldier adding to the torture of a crucified man by pushing a vinegar-soaked cloth into his mouth. The opposite is true – it's an act of kindness and great risk.*

The boy

He'd never seen a body nailed to wood. His friends talked, excited about it, but his mum and dad always made sure he didn't see. But the man who rode the donkey, he was going to be killed - even his parents couldn't hide that - so, when he heard what was going to happen, he decided to go. He wouldn't ask. It was a long way but not so far he couldn't get there and back again by evening. He didn't want to scare his mum and dad. He wasn't running away - he loved them but he knew they wouldn't let him go or take him and it was just, well, something pulled him. He remembered the man's kindness, the friendly men who came for the donkey (and how scared they'd been of mum), and he remembered that the man had talked to him like he was important - the way his mum and dad did but different because he didn't have to. He also remembered how his prayer had come out stronger at the evening meal, the Seder.

The road to the city was packed. The air was full of scuffed up dust from the road. Soldiers kept pushing at the crowd and shouting - most of the people, but not all, looked down and away from the soldiers who pushed, hard, with their red, curved, metal-embossed shields and jabbed with glinting swords. In the crowd he saw the potter from his village, a tall muscly man with curly black hair who smiled a lot and gave children pieces of soft clay to play with. He ran to the man – "can I walk with you?" The potter looked puzzled but put his hand on the boy's small shoulder as if to say, "yes you can, you'll be safe with me." They walked.

Later.

The sun still peeped and shone over the curves of the brown hills. High and low, birds flew home, fluffing and settling. The potter carried the boy, heavy, draped sleeping over his shoulder, arms lose and hanging around the big man's neck and back. The potters' feet crunched on the stones of the path to the house and the boys mum, sitting, scared, in the fading light, ran. She had been crying - her hands gripped a scarf wet with tears. The potter, smiling and sad at the same time, said, "I'll carry him in - show me where, please." Clutching her sleeping son's hand she led the potter to the child's bed on the floor. The boy's dad came in - he had been walking, looking, crazed, fearing that his child was lost. He was exhausted, edgy, gripped with worry, ready to be angry with, blame the potter, anybody, but his wife smiled, shook her head to quiet his fear and fury. She was always good at this.

The boy, settled, the adults went outside and sat. She brought wine and bread. The potter sat very still, hands resting on his thighs, holding a nearly spilling cup - he drank, a drop of red running from the corner of his mouth. "He asked me to look after him. I just thought he'd told you - he's always such a friendly, honest boy. I'm so, so sorry. He came all the way with me." The potter paused, put his cup down on the dry ground, dust stopping it tipping and gazed at them with a look like a flinch and a warning. "He saw, he watched the man Yeshua as he was nailed and hung up. I tried to turn him away, hide his face but he twisted to see. He's not my child; there was only so much I could do." She made a noise that was a hard pull of breath in and, with her hand then on her mouth, a moan of horror from her belly for her child with a wound she couldn't take away and hoped he'd never have. She and her husband grabbed each other's hands, hard, almost hurting. The potter left. needing to be with his wife, to hold her hands, put his arms close around his own children.

Later she fell asleep on the floor next to her child's bed. His hand had slipped out from the cover and rested on the floor, cool. She held it, carefully. She thought how soft, unmarked it was. As she floated between sleeping and waking, she wondered about the mother of the man who died - did she remember holding his small hand?

In the morning she woke and saw his bed, empty. For a moment terror flooded her, had she just dreamed he came home? Was he still lost? Then she heard, through the open door, the sound of a bucket banging against a manger, pouring food - he was feeding the donkeys, it was his job every morning. Quietly she dressed, walked to the well in the yard, wound the wobbling full bucket up and washed her hands and face splashing her clothes, the ground. Softly she stepped to the stable. The older donkey was sitting, legs folded, in thick straw. Her son had his arms around the donkey's neck, resting his head against hers, tears shaking him. She watched. Finally, he lifted up his head leaving a dark, damp stain on the donkey who shook and flicked her ears and settled to sleep.

She moved to his side, arms around him, their bodies fitting like always. He said he was sorry if he scared her and dad, but he'd had to go. Then he told her what he had seen and heard - the sound and look of a hammer, men laughing, dogs barking at the bottom of the wood. He said the man had looked sad like the day on the donkey but much, much, much more. "I tried to run to the big soldier hurting him with a spear to stop him, but the potter held me so tight I couldn't move and then, like some women very near and the potter, I cried and cried. Mum, he was kind, I liked him, why did they kill him?"

The women

The women, Miryam the mother, her cousin Salome, and Miryam from Magdala, stood to the edge of the crowd - at a corner close to the line of soldiers. Beronike, with her blood marked scarf, seeing them, not knowing who they were, stood close, an island of safety in the horror and they moved to make room. Their son, intimate friend, storyteller had been killed, a threat to everyone who listened to or loved him. The women were his last friends standing - all the men had fled.

The women were going to watch into the night, not leave for prayers - there were none left anyway; if priests prayed it would be like poison in wine.

Later.

Most watchers had gone, his death, in the end, was, for most, just like any other - even *he* had called out, abandoned, full of fear; another fighter killed and left hanging for the dogs already sniffing at his feet. The men, his other friends, had not come back, still terrified of the nails and spears. Beronike was the first to hear the sound of wheels. She saw the man with the beautiful cloak walking beside a cart pulled by a donkey with the bridle held by one of three men walking hunched, fear full. They came close to the women. Beronike stepped forward - the man in the gown paused then smiled remembering her kindness. "I can take him away from here, there is a tomb I can use but we have to be quick." Already the men were lifting a heap of rope from the cart. One man threw one end over the top of the upright beam and then two of them pulled and held the two ends, one each, in front of the dead man, tight. Carefully the third man sawed at the bottom of the wood until it was almost cut through, splintering - he pushed, and the rope holders gripped. The wood snapped and tipped back, the sawyer ran round putting his back under the burden, bracing as it lowered to the ground and stepping aside before it touched the earth.

The women, too stunned with pain to cry, holding hands, were a huddled block of red, blue, and brown cloth. They each closed their eyes whilst the men, weeping, tenderly worked the nails out. The bent broken legs came free, the hands next. The dead man's mum, Miryam, has brought the myrrh the travellers had given her all those years ago - she'd buried it carefully in its smooth, brown stone jar, ready for when it might ever be needed. Why did they give it? Maybe, she thought, for people travelling in the desert, death was always near - maybe myrrh had been a gift of truth and life as well as just something precious. She gave the myrrh to the man who brought the cart, pushes it quickly at him before the sun disappears into the night - when the body was wrapped the spice was folded into the layers of the cream cloth. The women can't touch the body, him, though their hands ache to help - a last touch, a mad idea that they might, just, be able to wake him. He's lifted softly, firmly held, as a baby might be, but dead, onto the cart.

Each person then walked holding the cart, the bridle or other harness-joined, afraid to let go. It would soon be dark. The women, too numb to be hungry, sadness filling them stagger, but don't fall.

Later

Exhausted by crying, aching in their bellies, they slept curled up together on the hard ground. Because they slept, they didn't see an old man, Josef, standing on a rise in the ground nearby, leaning on an old axe, held up by men either side of him, crying, as he keeps watch in case soldiers come. In the morning he is gone, again.

The women woke in the early sun, cold; for a moment they have forgotten what has happened and then they remembered and held onto each other as if they might fall and be lost.

There are many stories about what happened next.

He, their friend, son, storyteller, rabbi, was gone, dead, killed and there was a cold space in each of them where he'd been. It was like an abandoned cave, an empty tomb was in their middles, and they didn't know where to look to find him, to fill up again. They moved apart a little, wandering off, being with nobody. Then, in the solace of quiet, things happened.

One of the women, Miryam from Magdala, she'd been sitting in a tiny grove of trees and flowers nearby, stood quickly, startled, looked around her and then ran. Ran, ran like she could fly, to tell the men, returned, to come out, that she had seen him, heard him, leaned in the garden towards him to touch but couldn't and yet, somehow, felt him.

Miryam, his mother, dreamed, saw someone, something and she was awash with a deep peace inside like a running wave[27] through her, over her and then, still - she just sat resting against her cousin and friend Salome who had walked with her in the hush. The women each felt full again and asked, "what is this? How?"

27 There is a famous Celtic or Gaelic prayer that begins, 'Deep peace of the running wave to you....', and this bubbled up as I wondered about this story. https://www.worldprayers.org/archive/prayers/invocations/deep_peace_of_the_running.html

Fire in the night

There were two of them, a woman and a man, with their faces wrapped, hidden in cloth, just eyes shining. It was dark and a day after the story maker they loved had died, hammered on rough beams on the hill of bones. They crept, crouching sideways to the walls of buildings that glowed softly in the night light. Flinching at the clinking approach of soldiers who stepped in unison, they stopped, frightened almost to death, and edged into a shadowed alley. They waited. She touched his arm and they moved softly on from gap to gap, merging with the dark. Their hearts, they thought, were loud enough for anyone to hear. He remembered 'up here and then two more turns, left and right and we find it' – the yard full of timber. Their hurt, loss blazed in an anger that moved their legs.

Yesterday they had followed the man and his tormentors from the Temple to the street. They had seen who brought the cut wood for his death and dropped it, crashing, for him to lift, alone, almost breaking. They saw the bag of coins pass from the soldier to timber seller. They had left the crowds, for a little while, to follow the wagon to its yard and know where they would come back to for vengeance. They knew it wasn't what the man had taught but they just had to do something - for there to be consequences, cause, and effect.

Next to the yard was a stable, open. There was a trough against the wall and they stepped on its back edge and, bruising their bellies, stretched and pulled themselves over the top dropping into the unguarded yard. There were piles of once trees cut and trimmed, squared off ready for the next agonised deaths. If trees dream would this be their nightmare?

A sloping roof covered the long benches and sawing pit – the monster toothed saws and sharp scrapers hung on the walls. A rat rustled through heaps of wood shavings, ends of logs and mounds of sawdust. They piled spilling handfuls of scented curls and flakes under the racks of timber. Using a wooden shovel she heaped sawdust on the kindling – soft and powdery, dry and crisp. He balanced sawn off ends and bark on the fire bed. Pausing to breathe she looked at him, nodded with smiling eyes. He took the flints from a side slung bag and struck and struck until sparks flew and caught into small yellow flames. They knelt, blew and the flames grew and flared, hungry; leaning in they put more sawn tree and then tools into the blaze; hair on the backs of their hands singed and smelt. Grinning, they ran, using a leaning plank to scramble up and over the wall lowering themselves to step off the trough and flee home.

The soldiers, returning, began to run towards the high orange flickering glow yelling for help. People came out but were slow to bring buckets or fetch water.

Where is Emmaus? 28

Leaving the town, the old man, the trader, with his donkeys carrying bud shaped clay pots of deep red wine, weeps as he walks. He remembers years ago hearing the baby cry, talking to those shepherds, and feeling hope lift his heart. Now, there is another killed man, dead dream. He plods, silently, for miles, carrying sadness like extra baggage. Twilight makes bushes, trees, rocks look grey and hazy. He had hoped to reach the next village by nightfall, but the ache of grief has made him weary and slow. He stops, lights a small fire, lays out his food - bread, soft herby lentils and dates - and rests one of the pots of wine angled in the sandy soil - he wants the warm and spicy taste of the wine on his tongue.

In the stillness and quiet he hears footsteps and voices. Reaching for the pole that helps him walk and climb, thick and heavy, he stands, ready to fight if he has to. On the road above where he sits he sees two men appear round the big rock on the corner. He waits.

Earlier.

Aaron and Hezekiah are walking away from the town, the bottoms of their long robes grubby with dust and dung from the dry road. Aaron's face is bruised, purple, and nearly black on his left cheek with a web of small crusty cuts. He had been hit with a rough, splintery cudgel by a Temple guard helping the soldiers. Hezekiah limps - a grinning soldier had stamped on his foot and then kicked his shin. He had fallen and, for a few terrifying moments, the soldier had knelt on his neck. Aaron had tugged his friend away. They had shouted when a big soldier, a centurion, had speared their friend nailed to wood. They were lucky to get away.

They walk quickly, looking over their shoulders, hurrying, sometimes tripping, and reaching out to grab, hold and lift each other up. Coming to a rise in the road, the sun on their necks hot, their mouths thick and dry, tasting dirt and dust, they stop. Aaron pulls a clay bottle of wine and water from his bag, and they drink. He turns to his friend – "you said we're going to your cousins in Emmaus. Which Emmaus? I have a friend in Emmaus but it's not this way; it's the other side of the hill. Are you sure?" They look at each other, and, even in the middle of all their fear of being caught, punished, maybe killed, they smile and then, shaking their heads, begin to laugh and laugh so much their tummy muscles ache. Then tears they had not dared show pour like sudden thick rain and they have to hold onto each other, wrapped in a tangle of arms and shawl. Sitting for a moment, Aaron says, "here we are, running away and we don't know where we're going, fleeing like scared sheep. Let's walk some more, find a place to rest and decide what to do tomorrow." Hezekiah, always quieter than his friend, just says, "yes" softly but he is glad, relieved after their panicked rush that they can see and say they are exhausted, confused and lost - without blaming or attacking one another. Good friends.

After a few more miles the sun slips behind the hills, the past they are walking from dipped in shadow. They are going slowly now: the fear leaked away. They talk quietly about the friends they'd left when they fled - are they safe, where have they hidden, is everybody, somehow, together or is everyone scattered? They came to a huge boulder marking a curve in the road. Going round it, they see, lower down, a man standing in front of a row of sitting donkeys. He stands feet apart, holding a thick stave. They paused and wave - they've seen him lots of times before, always leading a line of pack animals heavy with pots, bags, sacks or bundles. Aaron calls, "I'm Aaron and this is my friend Hezekiah - we're trying to get away from the trouble in the town. We're a bit lost." It was a risk saying all this. The trader, Ezra, smiles, puts his pole against a rock and waves to them to come down.

The air grows quickly cold, and they sit on the ground near the fire. Beginning to talk about the terrible day they have each been in they drink a little wine glad of its warm flow in their mouths. A dusky thrush sings its ending song for the day, and they pause to listen. Ezra's head flicks up, again alert to the sound of footsteps. A tall man walking with long strides is on the road. He stops, looks at them, checking, and then seeing Ezra's kind wave comes down, slipping a little, joining them by the fire.

Aaron, Hezekiah, and the stranger lay out their food with Ezra's. They are all hungry. They eat and drink, gladly passing more food to one another.

Some years later.

Aaron speaks:

"My wife and I and our children - there are three, two girls and a boy - live with lots of other families in a small group of houses by a spring in the hills, it's called Emmaus, away from the road used by soldiers. My friend, Hezekiah, is here sometimes - he travels about a lot talking to people about our little village and how we live. Yes, he talks a lot now! How we've all changed. I'm a miller - a donkey turns the stone to grind the grain to make the flour for my neighbours and others nearby.

I think often about that evening when we were running away, not sure where to, in danger. So many people were and are still living in hazard. Then, I was a frightened, angry, disappointed younger man whose friend, teacher & confidante, had been killed brutally & mercilessly. Ezra, the trader, and the eldest of us around the fire, had talked about his sadness, told us the story of the time he had heard the baby crying, talking to the men in the town and those in the hills guarding sheep, hearing them sing in the distance, sure of new days coming. As he talked, I felt safer. The evening darkened. I told Ezra and the stranger what had happened to us and asked, furiously, what had been the G'd forsaken point of everything we had seen, heard, and helped with. The men of power, greed, deceit, and cruelty were still in charge. People were still hungry, poor, scared - nothing had changed, nothing. It was then, I remember, that I began to feel strange, uneasy, and uncomfortable inside, like something was pushing its way up in me. Talking afterwards the others said that I had gone quiet, somehow away from them.

An owl hoohoo'd from a tree higher up the hill. Breaking the hush around the fire, the stranger slowly reached for the last small, round loaf. I thought, 'oh, he's still hungry - it's good we were here.' Gently he broke off four pieces of the beautiful bread - gave one each to me, Hezekiah, and Ezra and kept the last for himself. He poured, for each of us, a little wine that had been decanted into a silvery metal jug with a high curved handle and long pointed spout - it was precious to Ezra; it had been his mother's and had been used only on holy or very special days. The stranger had become the host. He asked me, 'Aaron, what might you change?', and, after a pause, 'what did your friends' stories make you feel you could do?' and then, 'what are you hiding from?' As he spoke, he dipped his bread in his wine and ate it - Hezekiah, Ezra and I did the same. It was as if, in the moment, it was more than just food and drink and, somehow, had become all the food and drink there had ever been, that you would be glad of and could share with others whilst you ate and drank. Somehow embodying love."

The flames and shadows of the fire flickered over the stranger's face and, as in a short, stark dream on the borders of sleep or a bright, trembling mirage seen, alone, in a hot desert, Aaron glimpsed, there, the shape of his dead friend's face. He gasped, shook his head. He remembered the touch of his friend's look and the feeling of coming home when he listened, with the others, to the man's stories without end. Inside he felt like dough before it became bread - pummelled, broken, and kneaded and then left to change visibly and invisibly. He said nothing and sat very still. A nightjar roiled out its song somewhere from its hollow in the ground, a fast, chinking bubbling that reminded them it was night-time. They each left the circle of the fire and, wrapped in blankets, lay to sleep.

In the morning the air was cold and smelt of the damp, extinguished, scattered fire. The stranger was gone. Ezra, feeling lighter in his step, gave his animals, his constant company, grain and water. Aaron, chewing a last piece of bread, looked at Hezekiah and said, with a long deep breath slowly in and out, "I'm going back." Hezekiah smiled.

28 Emmaus. The stimulus for this story was an anecdote from Marcus Borg. He said that, with Marianne Borg and two other friends, he had gone to a chapel or museum commemorating the Emmaus story. It was shut but the caretaker said, "don't worry, there's another one down the road that might still be open"

The old woman and a star²⁹

There's a man called Benjamin.

Benjamin speaks:

"I'm visiting a small village tucked between low hills away from military roads. I'd heard that the people here are trying to live differently, do something new. Let me tell you about the most memorable day of my visit. An aged woman, my host, sat, resting on cushions, in a curved dark wood chair. She smiled and sipped some of the new wine from her neighbour's vines. Small, brown birds hopped, pecking crumbs from the packed earth just inside the open door - sun-warmed air stroked early morning chill off her arms. She ate a little bread. I sat eating, waiting for her to answer my questions - I'd asked so many already.

Sitting back, she began. "The idea of the star? That was mine" she said. "You see, the disappointment, sadness, was so huge. Things didn't get better and the man we thought would change everything didn't come back to make it happen, do it all for us. We remembered that when he spoke it was often sort of sideways, in pictures or puzzles leading each of us to a hidden treasure that loves to be found, working it out for ourselves. We talked and talked about what stories might help us, tell others that when he spoke, what he did, was like a welcome fire by the road in the evening, a star in a black night sky or, depending how dark things were for you, a candle lit in a cell or a cave. I'd heard something about a star that flew through the sky near the time he was born, and I thought, 'we'll use that - perfect'. You ask about the travellers - oh they definitely came, and they had the most wonderful gifts, but more about them later."

She stood, stretched carefully. She said the warm wine had eased the pain in her knees and hips and that she must thank her neighbour again. Smiling, she said, almost to herself, "he's such a tall, handsome man and he's so shy I really shouldn't flirt with him but, well, why not - it cheers me up and makes the other women smile and the men nervous." She grinned and apologised. Remembering something half forgotten, she said, "I must pick the beans before they become too hard." She went outside.

I sat finishing fruit and bread.

When she came back in from her luscious green garden, she was holding a basket full of beans mottled pink and red. They needed to be rinsed in water from a jug, swirled in a big clay bowl for dust and pieces of plant to float away and be skimmed off. Then they had to be spread out on a big cloth, gleaming, to dry. When that was all done it was, she said, "nearly time to eat again – it's going to be crowded; we can talk more later. Maybe, though, if I tell a story that will help you."

Soon the little square house with three rooms and big doors was full. Children, babies, mums, dads, sisters, brothers, cousins, friends and neighbours, older people like the woman - all glad of company and food to share. The cloth on the floor was covered with bread, salted fish, fruit and cooked beans, honey and cheese. Everybody ate, passing food to each other - seeing to other people's wants before their own.

I was a stranger from another village made welcome. Friends at home had said it would be safe to visit these people and good to listen to their stories, but I didn't know how they did things. I started to get bowls ready for cleaning, but a man, smiling, tapped my arm and pointed to the floor, "sit, sit and see what happens next."

The woman, back in her chair, picked up a little child and settled them on her lap. "Shall I tell you a story?" Small hands clapped together, and each face smiled. "This is a story with a very looong name - it's called the story of five riders, two kings, a mum, and a baby. I'll begin".[29]

"Once there was a king who lived in a palace made of rock - it looked like part of a cliff. Now, the king had a daughter. He told her she had to marry a man who called himself a king. He wasn't really but was very rich with a big army of soldiers. If she married him, it might stop his army fighting her dad's. She did marry him, but he was horrible and, later, she had to run away back home. It's not always easy being a princess! Meanwhile, years before she had to run away, her dad heard a story about someone being born, near where she lived, who might be a new chieftain, maybe a king or even a wise and clever person like in the old days." A small voice called out, "Like you Booba?" The old woman smiled and carried on. "The story wasn't about a warrior with an army - it was about a baby. He heard it from one of the people who rode horses through the desert with lines of camels carrying all sorts of lovely things for other people to buy - perfume, oil, and cloth, spices of all sorts, beans, and fruit. Now", she said, "before I say more about what happens next there is something very important you need to know. A long, long time ago the people who lived in this king's country had lived in the desert, never stopping anywhere for more than a few days. They had a treasure that they looked after and, sometimes, hid from others but they never forgot all the places that they hid it - deep in the sand, secretly behind rocks. This treasure made them safe, rich and never hungry. Can you guess what it was?" One of the men listening to the story smiled. He travelled a lot and knew the answer but didn't say. Voices called out, 'gold, spices, wine, jewels, swords and spears, camels' - and more. She smiled. "All good ideas but, no. It was water, just water. Without the treasure of water, they couldn't cross the desert and mountains. With the water they could plant and grow food and the more they grew the more they had to sell or give to others. They stopped moving all the time. Even when they became rich and never hungry, they didn't forget the treasure of a simple thing and knew how precious everything could be. Like a new baby. Remember this idea of a hidden treasure.

The king in the palace of rock was puzzled. What should he do about this new baby? What would his daughter's husband do? Our king liked to know things, but he knew he couldn't know everything - that was clever, but he still felt a bit funny, not sure what to do."

The old woman paused to sip some water, and another small voice said, "oh please don't stop - what did the king do?"

"Aaaaah now. I was coming to that. So, elsewhere, and nearby in a deep cave that was like a temple into which the sun shone and touched patterns and pictures on the walls on different days and times of the year, an old man sits. The room where he sits has been cut out of the rock and is quiet around him, lit by several small round clay lamps burning oil through a spout. He's sitting on a dark blue rug with cushions behind him, his back against the wall. A jug full of flowers - roses and jasmine - perfumes the warm air. He's alone. His beard is thick, white and soft. He sits very, very still. His head is covered with a creamy coloured shawl like a small soft blanket - it also wraps his shoulders - cosy. In his lap, cradled in the cloth of his gown, is a scroll, a book written on long paper rolled up around a dark carved wooden stick. From the ends of the stick hang red and gold strings dangling with tassels. He's reading from the scroll quietly speaking each word as his finger moves just above the paper. He frowns a little, looks puzzled like he's digging with his thoughts. A few days ago, a star had flashed across the sky with a big, shining, bright tail behind it. It sparkled. Stars always made him smile. Surprise stars made him smile more and also think about things bigger than him and reminded him there was always mystery and magic and interesting things going to happen.

"This old man was a story holder. His job, and that of women and men like him, was to know stories of what other people had done over a long, long time and remember and keep them safe. They would tell them so the people who heard, children, women, men, like all of you, would remember and the story would not be lost, and it might help them with hard or complicated problems and worries. Today the king came for help, alone and quiet. The man listened to the king's puzzle.

'I have also heard about this baby' he said. 'I've been reading, looking back at old, old words.' He touched, almost stroked the scroll on his lap. 'Did you know that this baby is born where the people, the tribe, called the Jews live? Their oldest books say that one day a person will be born who will change everything - it will be, as they say, a Jubilee, when slaves will be free, no one will be hungry or poor, debts will be gone, and war will end. Everybody will come to the greatest feast. I wonder how your daughter's husband will feel about that. I hear he likes to be rich and will take whatever he wants from people just for himself and that he can be very, very cruel. You are the king here and can do what you want but you know there are snakes hiding in some men's hearts just like they do in the desert waiting to bite and feed. Oh, I know you can make your soldiers fight and die in battles if you want to, but I think you would rather not. Watch out for the snakes.' Some of the children snuggled up to their mums.

"The king was quiet. He loved talking with and listening to the story holder - somehow answers to his questions and worries flowed like water over rocks without his having to think and think. He knew what to do and thanked the man, promising to send food and wine."

Here the old woman stopped again, looking around at everybody. She beckoned with her hand for the listeners to come closer. "Now," she said, "some days later there were five horses waiting - bells tinkling when they shook their heads, empty saddles, polished with riding and care, shiny and brown. Behind them, roped together, were two camels, loaded up with parcels and clay bottles wrapped and tied in straw. They were munching from bags of food hanging from their necks - they had a long journey coming. The camels were not near the horses, their strong, hairy, musty smell scared them.

The five riders of the horses sat inside a deep red, many pointed tent. Swirling gold-threaded patterns glimmered on its roof and sides. They sat, women and men, on cushions and rugs spread across the red cloth floor. They ate soft bread and olives, drinking water. They listened to the king who stood next to the story holder who sat on a chair with gold patterned cushions. Still.

The king said, 'You will be very careful. I will give you gifts for my daughter and the king and also gifts for the family of the baby we hear has been born. The king may be angry about this - remember, he is a very dangerous, cruel man. You will have to find the palace where the baby lives - I don't know.'

Beside the king was a low square table covered with a shiny, silky purple cloth. Nestled on top of the cloth were two small and one bigger, round-glazed clay jars with stoppers tied with dried grasses. Next to these were a red cloth bag and a small green glass bottle sealed with a golden cap. The king said, 'the bottle is perfume of roses for my daughter. One of the small jars concerns scented unguent for healing the king's discomfort - on one of the camels there is good wine for him too. Hulda, you will take the perfume.' A woman stood, came to the king who, carefully, gave her the bottle. Wrapping it in a sky-blue cloth she softly put it in a bag slung across her shoulders and hanging at her side; walking backwards she bowed her head and sat. 'Rabbel,' the king said, 'you will take the unguent and make sure the wine, all of it, is delivered.' Rabbel, a man, stood, smiling, and the other four riders laughed quietly - Rabbel loved wine. He came to the king, took the small jar and also bowing his head walked backwards to sit again. The king paused and the story holder stood to speak. 'We find ourselves in the middle of someone else's story and we cannot know the part we play but we, or you, will play it anyway. What gifts can you give to someone who may be a chieftain, a king or even a wise and clever person like in the old days?' He picked up the red cloth bag and shook it - there was a metal chinking sound. 'First there is gold. Gold always helps and it also says we wish you riches and good things.' He picked up the last small clay jar. 'This jar holds oil of frankincense - the scent of angels. It will remind his parents and, later, him that G'd is always near.' He picked up the bigger jar and looked around, almost sad. 'This is a gift of something else true. Illness can come as can death. This is myrrh to heal or to add to the cloth that wraps a body. It is a medicine and also a reminder that things end, always.' Some mothers held their children closer. Stepping forward the story holder gave the gifts to the last three riders and then sat. The king smiled at him and said to the riders, 'just try to say what we have said and watch so, so carefully what happens and listen with your desert ears.' Looking at each of the riders he smiled and then left to eat, rest, wonder and talk with his friend the story holder. The riders left. There was whinnying and stamping from the horses as they felt the riders' excitement - the camels, joined by long ropes to the backs of two of the riders' saddles, coughed and grumbled. The sounds faded into the silence of the sand.

It was many, many days before the riders returned tired, dirty, and hungry. They'd rushed. Sitting in the red tent again they told the king and the story holder what had happened. 'I gave your daughter the perfume and she smiled like the sun rising but then became sad and silent' Hulda said. One of the other riders, a man, Malichus, his face burned dark brown by the sun with deep creases like carved gullies in rock, smiled at the king. 'We told Herod that his gifts were for friendship - he seemed to be always scratching and thanked us for the unguent. The wine, all of it, went straight to his store - cool, down steep steps underground. I said we were also hoping to find and give welcome gifts to this new baby we had heard of. You told us to watch and listen. Well,' Malichus said, 'I remember seeing a snake in the desert and, as it rose up to bite me and before I moved swiftly away, it looked like it was smiling - Herod's face was like that. After that we left. We are brave, all of us, but we felt unsure, unsafe.'

'Now,' the king asked, 'did you find the child? Where was it?' Malichus spoke again looking a bit worried but still smiling. 'Oh yes, we found him. He was in a barn behind a small caravanserai - an old trader with mules told us where to look. The parents were there - his dad, a carpenter, and the mother, who was very young. It was odd. We thought they might be frightened but they just made us welcome - shared a little food and water. Peculiarly, it was the most peaceful I have felt in a long time.' The story holder nodded and also smiled as if he knew something secret but didn't say. The king laughed. 'In a barn? What happened to the gifts?' Malichus spoke, 'well, we said what the story holder said - the mother, her name was Miryam, smiled, cried in a quiet way and thanked us as she put the gifts on the straw covered floor near to the baby who was lying awake in a feeding box. The father, his name was Yosef, first looked puzzled and then sort of safe, relieved - they were very poor you see. We told them Herod was dangerous and that they should leave or hide and tell other families also. Then, we were so surprised, she carefully lifted the baby up and said would we like to hold him - I looked around and wondered whether my friends here had, like me, felt tears come to their eyes. When I held the child, for a moment I didn't ever want to let go. When Miryam held him again she opened the frankincense and dabbed it on the baby's forehead - the warm air was filled with the scent, and it clung to my clothes for a while after.'

Thanked by the king the riders left, bowing. The king looked at the story holder - 'in a barn, this new chieftain or king or wise person you read of was in a barn not a palace. We must watch closely to see what happens.'

The old woman, finished speaking, took a small bottle from a low, round, pale wood table beside her, opened it and, with her finger over its top, tipped it - her fingertip came away glistening. She stood slowly, stiff, and touched each child on their forehead with scented oil. Everybody breathed in the sweet, musky aroma and smiled. Some parents stood to get fruit and drinks for everyone. No one wanted to leave - it was like they were all gathered in.

The old woman turned, gazing at me, her round brown face smoothed. Long loose threads of grey hair dangled down her cheeks, "Of course, she said, "stories have to be brighter and more beautiful and strange than completely true, but they did come, I remember. I was there, you see. It was me who helped Miryam when the baby came." I gasped and my heart filled, ached and my eyes spilled. She smiled at me when I finally looked up. I stroked the tears from my cheeks and eyelashes and sat still.

29 Weaving a new story away from the traditional 'wise men' was one of the hardest components of this work until I found writing by Dwight D Longenecker about Nabatean traders. This gave me a nudge out of the 2,000-year-old narrative. Here's a link: https://dwightlongenecker.com/identified-the-wise-

Epilogue
*settings, audience,
and influences*

I have left thoughts about who these stories are for, where and how you might use them and what has influenced their formation until this epilogue. We're so used to being told how we should do or use something that our trust in our intuition and spontaneity can be eroded. I am interested in the fertility of the imagination and how that can be nurtured. I like the idea of there being a storyteller in each of us. I have been learning about how fungal, mycelial underground networks in woods invisibly grow, how they link and nourish whole ecologies and are, equally, fed in return. I think story can do the same for our interior lives and for the different communities that we belong to. We can evoke memory and reinvigorate kindness and courage; we can learn how generations before us have grappled with difficulties and experienced joy and hope. Other people's narratives can, unexpectedly, open us to our own.

What settings are these stories for? Well, wherever it occurs to you that you might read or tell them – wherever they might be interesting or useful in your personal, family, community, political, religious, or working life. My intention is that readers first encounter the stories and then have their own thoughts about when they might use them, if at all.

What ages are these stories for? The stories are for a wide range of ages and not only adults. Some are definitely suitable for young children although most are for people aged 10 and beyond. It is important to recognise that, saying the stories are suitable 'for people aged 10 and beyond' does not mean that they are somehow 'childish' or less than 'adult'. People of any age have great capacity for the wondering, wisdom and learning that these stories can evoke. The main limitation is where narratives are particularly harsh or cruel or, once, about a sex worker; but even this is complicated. Adults have to face the challenge of how to have conversations with children about difficult or frightening things. Children need to feel that they can ask questions or express thoughts or feelings without being closed down or ignored.

So, I suggest, pay heed to your audience, even if it is just you, one person or many, adjust language as necessary but remember that people of all ages can be more resilient and have better protective filters than you might imagine. Of course, don't be casual or careless in your telling and allow, if necessary, for someone to say, 'I don't want to hear anymore just now.' It is also worth recalling, when thinking about children, that unsanitised folk and fairy stories and much contemporary children's literature can be dark, grotesque and frightening but also rich in archetypes and day to day parallels.

It can be helpful to have reflective questions ready to use if you are telling these stories to others. They can also be helpful privately as a focus. I think some very effective open questions for this purpose come from a widely used approach to theological reflection called *Godly Play©*. The questions to invite thinking and personal, existential engagement include:

- I wonder, which part of this story do you like the best?
- I wonder, which part of this story do you think is most important?
- I wonder if there is any part of this story that you are in or is in you?
- I wonder if there is any part of this story that you could leave out and still have all the story that you need?

If you use these questions with others, accept people's responses without comment other than affirming that their words have been heard – hard to do but validating for whoever speaks. If a response includes a question or further wondering, reflect it back to the speaker before responding yourself. These wondering questions are simple but powerful tools. Again, using them is not a requirement.

What influenced my writing?

The stories began life when I was Children's Work Officer for Quakers in Britain. Much of my work focussed on equipping adults to explore complex moral, theological, and social issues with children. Within this sat questions about how to help children grapple with reflective and non-literal approaches to the bible. There were only a few stories to help with this, so a project 'big stories for small people' began – 'Ohh… but listen' grew out of that.

The thinking and writing of three American theologians has been a big help. The late Marcus J Borg, John Dominic Crossan and Walter Wink were members of the Jesus Seminar. This was a network of Christian academics and teachers active from the 1980s to the early 21st century. The task that the network took on was to explore, in lay persons terms, the question, 'who was the historical Jesus?' This exploration led the Seminar and a widening circle of others to consider how looking at who he might have been affects thinking now about spirituality, social justice and contemporary religious practice. Working on 'Ohh…but listen' I was, intuitively, already engaged with all of those different themes – the depth of the thinking and the risk taking of these writers provided me with deeper, stronger frameworks.

Particular books by the three writers include:

Meeting Jesus again, for the first time – Marcus J Borg; *HarperSanFrancisco;* ISBN 0-06-060916-7

The Heart of Christianity – Marcus J Borg; *HarperSanFrancisco*; ISBN 0-06073068-4

The First Christmas – Marcus J Borg and John Dominic Crossan; *HarperOne*; ISBN 978-0-06-143071-8

The Last Week - Marcus J Borg and John Dominic Crossan; *SPCK*; ISBN 978-0-281-05983-6

The Powers that be: Theology for a New Millennium - Walter Wink; *Harmony*; ISBN 0-38-548752-5

An article from the *Lutheran Peace Fellowship on Walter Wink and Nonviolence:* https://www.lutheranpeace.org/articles/transcript-of-walter-winks-nonviolence-for-the-violent

Whilst working with Quakers wasn't always easy, the practice of simply linking the love, the divine if you like, that is accessible in most of us, though not all, to how we live and act in the world underpins this work. It is, of course, not limited to one faith or belief group. Mutual aid, kindness, compassion, resilience and goodness belong to no one but remain available to anyone who chooses.

Finally, through practice and risk I discovered and trusted that I can tell stories.

On the shingle shore of the town of Aldeburgh in Suffolk, England is a large rugged and beautiful steel sculpture of a scallop shell by sculptor Maggi Hambling. The scallop is an old symbol of pilgrimage. Cut out of the top edge of part of the shell are words from a poem by George Crabbe that are also used in the Benjamin Britten opera *Peter Grimes:* "I hear those voices that will not be drowned".

STORY WORKS